Murdo MacDonald-Bayne was born the son of a farmer. He had his first as a small boy, after which he found he could see and hear things that others couldn't. Another particularly profound spiritual experience occurred when he was badly wounded and left for dead during the Battle of the Somme in the First World War. He received the British War Medal, the Victory Medal and the Military Cross. In the early 1930s, he founded The College of Universal Science in Manchester, England where he taught metaphysics, going on to establish a centre in Johannesburg, South Africa, where he received the teachings that appear in this book. Married with children, Murdo MacDonald-Bayne was awarded with doctorates in Divinity and Philosophy in later life. He died in 1955.

By the same author:

The Higher Power You Can Use

I am the Life

Heal Yourself

Spiritual and Mental Healing

What is Mine is Thine (How to use Your Divine Power)
Parts I and II

How to Relax and Revitalize Yourself

DIVINE HEALING OF MIND AND BODY

The Master Speaks Again...

Murdo MacDonald-Bayne, MC, PhD, DD

RIDER

LONDON · SYDNEY · AUCKLAND · JOHANNESBURG

This edition reissued in 2013 by Rider,
an imprint of Ebury Publishing

First published in Great Britain in 1953 by L N Fowler & Co, and
reissued in 1999 by C W Daniels Ltd

Ebury Publishing is a Random House Group company

The Random House Group Limited Reg. No. 954009

Addresses for companies within the Random House Group can
be found at: www.randomhouse.co.uk

A CIP catalogue record for this book is
available from the British Library

The Random House Group Limited supports The Forest Stewardship
Council® (FSC®), the leading international forest certification
organisation. Our books carrying the FSC label are printed on FSC®
certified paper. FSC is the only forest certification scheme endorsed by
the leading environmental organisations, including Greenpeace.
Our paper procurement policy can be found at:
www.randomhouse.co.uk/environment

MIX
Paper from
responsible sources
FSC® C016897

Printed and bound in Great Britain by Clays Ltd, St Ives plc

ISBN 9780852073322

Copies are available at special rates for bulk orders. Contact the sales
development team on 020 7840 8487 for more information.

To buy books by your favourite authors and register for offers, visit:
www.randomhouse.co.uk

CONTENTS

FOREWORD

IT would be impossible for me to explain how these talks were given, for I would only be giving my opinion which might be incorrect, but I can tell you of the feelings I had.

For several months prior to the giving of these talks I would awaken from my sleep at night hearing a voice apparently speaking in me. I thought I was dreaming yet it was not a dream, it was a real voice, whether it was my own or another I cannot say. The peculiar thing was that I could hear this voice and reason what it said at the same time.

After many of these experiences the voice said that special talks would be given when the proper time arrived. The time did arrive and the voice spoke instructing that the talks would begin on a certain night when those attending were all chosen. Thereafter no one must be allowed in during the series of talks, also that these talks must be taken down in shorthand and must also be recorded on a wire recorder so that nothing would be lost.

When the night for those talks duly arrived I took my place in the auditorium, I was quite concerned about what was going to happen, when I felt as if 1,000 volts of electricity were passing through me. I did not lose consciousness although I became aware of a magnificent power, a consciousness far above my own. Yet we seemed to be linked together in some mysterious way, which I cannot explain because I do not know.

Then I could hear my voice yet it was different, speaking with great authority, an authority of one who absolutely knew. I listened very attentively to what was said and could understand with a clarity that I never had before. The language was perfect without a flaw, without a hesitation, for a whole hour this went on, I was amazed because I knew that no human brain could duplicate such a feat, yet this feat was repeated each week for fourteen weeks.

Only when I heard the talks on the wire recorder did I know that something strangely beautiful had taken place. I wondered and I am still wondering about the wonder of it all. You can read for yourselves what was said and if it gives you the comfort and satisfaction that it gave me and also those who had the privilege of hearing these spoken words, then they have not been spoken in vain.

Not one word has been added nor has one word been taken away.

*   *   *   *   *

A few of the many experiences of the students who were present have been recorded in the next few pages.

M. MACDONALD-BAYNE.

TALKS GIVEN THROUGH DR. MACDONALD-BAYNE

Description given by Miss I. Bagot-Smith

A TRANSFIGURATION EXPERIENCE NEVER TO BE FORGOTTEN

IN the spring of 1948 a series of talks was given in .... To those who were chosen to hear them, this was a unique and unforgettable experience. No one who heard them could ever be the same again. They were hours of the highest spiritual growth and understanding. It was as though a veil were torn from our eyes and we could see clearly. The veritable presence of the Master became so strong a reality to us that it has never faded but grown in intensity and vividness. And always, since that time, when we lift our minds to spiritual things, suddenly we know the Master is beside us, the Power of the Father is within and all is well.

It was not the actual words that made these lectures so amazing ; it was the way they were delivered. The words themselves will ring in our memories for ever, but the greatest Truth was shown to us without words, and no description could ever convey the tremendous force of the Presence of the Master, and, through him, the Love of the Father—a distinct evidence more real than anything physical around us.

As the lecturer entered, he was the kindly, smiling man we all knew so well. After a pause of silence, he seemed to breathe himself out of his body in a sudden gasp, leaving it swaying and without control. Then suddenly an amazing change took place : a short, sharp intake of breath and the very Master was present, in the same body, but utterly different. We knew perfectly well that the lecturer was still the man we had all known and respected for years, but at the same time he was someone completely different. The change was so startling that our benumbed senses could scarcely credit it. But at the same time it was true, and we knew it was true. The man before us now appeared unusually tall, much taller than the lecturer himself. Words cannot tell the strength of this astounding truth—but it was so. We were forced to believe it beyond the evidence of our ordinary senses.

Here now before us was a man, commanding of aspect, austere and of great authority, with brilliant eyes and an assurance of power. Straight and tall he stood before us and with deep solemnity he pronounced his regular greeting :—

" My peace I bring to you."

As the speaker progressed and we became more understanding, the greeting changed to "My peace and my love I bring to you," " My peace and my blessings I bring to you."

The blessing was given with the two first fingers of the right hand raised in the manner of a king, and low our hearts bowed before its majesty.

A quietness spread through the hall : a vibrating power like a stream of warmth passed through our bodies, burning wherever any part was imperfect, and healing as it flowed.

As one talk followed the other, we could feel our own vibrations raised and our understanding clarified and lifted to a plane far beyond our everyday life. In dawning comprehension we listened to truths greater than any we had ever heard, and yet—to our wondering astonishment —we realised they were the same statements we had heard and read since infancy. But only now did we understand their meaning. Suddenly the lightning truth flashed into our minds and at last we knew the power of what the Master had first said so many years ago. And then his truths became, for us, Reality, part of our very being, to be held precious in a golden silence from now on into Eternity.

Each word fell deliberately, with never a moment of hesitation, almost like drops of water or jewels falling one after another into the pool of silence deep around us. Each sentence was of perfect construction, spoken effortlessly and with no pause for thought,

Gradually we came to know quite simply and without wonder that we were not the only people present. Among us were those whom we loved, who had passed on ahead, while beyond them, in ever-widening circles, ranged thousands of higher entities.

The Master would address us all together and then, in regard to the deeper things of life, we would be given just what each could grasp. We in earthly bodies were addressed as " You of mortal sense," while the Master would raise his eyes and speak directly to those who had lately passed on as to minds who had gained in breadth of perception, who now knew the joy of a plane more spiritual and lovely and infinitely free. And then in awe we listened while the Master spoke to those who had more nearly approached his highest perfection. High above us we felt them, and far behind us, row upon row ; but no one moved or turned a head as our eyes were held by the Master. Our bodies had long since faded from our senses —they were simply in abeyance, glued into immobility, as it were, and it would take a definite effort to move them in any way.

The Master would bless us each in turn, first us " of mortal sense " and then the Spirits advanced so high above

us, and his voice would warm to their greater perception.
In us he perceived a rooted sense of separation, in them
a unity that was a relief and a joy to him. How small we
felt—how utterly unworthy !—tiny, lowly people, almost
infants, reaching up uncomprehending hands to what was
still a mystery. But gradually we grew in the stature of
our own minds and our own self-respect. In daily life
we found ourselves leading where before we had stepped
diffidently back—our voice came with unexpected assurance and authority. We too seemed to grow taller and to
tread more lightly as if the spirit-self were growing
stronger than the physical self.

Some of us saw glorious colours behind the lecturer :
waves of purple and gold so glowing that it almost hurt
the eyes. To some a slantwise cross was visible, to some
a thick shaft of brilliant white light pouring into the top
of his head, while many saw the long red-gold hair and
beard, while heavenly music and bells were heard in the
background as he spoke.

It became increasingly clear to us that the Master had
come to give us his age-old message : " I come to show
you the Father."

How often we had heard it before, but with blinded
senses. Now we began to understand.

We learnt of the Master Jesus, himself a man as we
were, highly sensitive, developed, perceiving, aware, as
we were not, of the wonder of the Christ within, the Son
of the Living God. He and the Christ and his Father were
one Being. Of himself he could do nothing ; but, identified
with the Christ, one with the Father, he could do all
things and have dominion over all things.

As the talks commenced, his voice was always grave
and austere, as from a distance, sure and firm as a great
leader speaking to followers searching for knowledge.
But, as he talked, his voice warmed to us, his eyes shone

with lovingness, his delight in our response and in the understanding of his Spirit.

The listeners grew more and more. And now and then, in speaking of the Father he would be overcome with his own emotion of the love so aroused. His voice would fade away and, entirely forgetful of us, suddenly he would so lose himself in the Love of the Father that it was as though an actual Being were between us. He spoke to one much nearer than we were : to someone so close as to be " nearer than breathing." He would stand wrapped in the glory of the Godhead. He would murmur directly to his Father. Sometimes we heard the words, " Father, I love Thee, I love Thee, and I love those that Thou hast given me—Thy children. I thank Thee for them." In the pause his face was lit with a love of ineffable tenderness ; a light of pure ecstasy transfigured his features, almost blinding in its intensity ; our eyes could not bear the brilliance that shone from his face. It was as though he had entered into some holy Temple of Love such as we could not comprehend. In awe we gazed—the Presence of the Father so strong, so tangible, so vivid, as to be far more real than the people around us. They faded ; he was there strong, powerful, in glory beyond glory.

And we too began to know the Father—an actively loving Being : no mere passive Godhead but a Father, powerful in guidance, in achieving all the Son could wish, a loving Father with arms around him, sheltering him in an ecstasy of peace.

A love shone through his presence, embracing all of us, impartially, universally, forcing us to realise the Truth as a Truth real beyond anything that could be touched or seen—the Truth of the Presence of God—a loving, active, positive, dynamic Father, a silent partner, at our shoulder always, a God who travelled home with us, came in at the gate with us, protecting us, so that for evermore no fear would enter into our homes or lives. The Love of the Father became an unmistakable reality. No words of the Master gave us that realisation ; it was his own intense, burning, joyful love of the Father that forced this knowledge upon us. And, because of this belonging to the Father, the Son was filled with a peace and a glory of happiness that was eternal and infinite.

And as he ascended again to his Father, he called us his disciples and he left with us his assurance :

" My peace, and my love, my blessings, I leave with you to remain with you."

At the time we felt that that was the end, and we longed for the wonder of the talks over again. But twice more he came, with a space of several months between.

At these times he spoke differently, bidding us search our hearts to see how much we had progressed along the path of Love that he had shown us. He asked us : " Is your faith so great that now you too could walk upon the water ? " And again, " Does your love for the Father order all your thoughts and deeds ? " " Do you live in love to the exclusion of all else ? "

How deeply shamed we felt at the little we had done, and how unworthy we knew ourselves to be of the honour of his coming.

*   *   *   *   *

The speaker continues to lecture week by week, and often the Master, quite visibly, takes over his body for an amazing moment, just at the end to give us his solemn blessing. The transfiguration is complete, with gown, face, beard and hair showing through the brilliant light around him,

" My love and my peace remain with you."

So that, in daily life, we know that the Master is beside us, and reverently we tread the earth, we whom he called his disciples, with the sure knowledge, in our hearts, of the undying Christ, alive and present in the world to-day.

Mrs. Patterson says :

" Words are inadequate to express what I saw and felt when our Master spoke to us through the Doctor. For a few seconds I was aware of a silence, unlike anything I had ever experienced ; it seemed that I was suddenly transported into another world. Then I saw the whole outline of the Doctor's body change ; his face took on quite a different expression and beams of light radiated from him. The face of the Master showed up clearly.

" The auditorium was charged with Power and Light.

" At the time I did not realise it, but a great change took place within myself. I was left with a deep feeling of security in a Living Christ, which is everything to me."

Mrs. Gilbert, a medium who travelled the world, states :

" I have been a medium for over thirty years, but I have never witnessed anything like I saw with the transfiguration of the Master. The Light that shone from him was so great that I had to close my eyes. I have never heard music so clearly before. The Auditorium was filled with those who had gone on before us. What joy it was to listen to the voice that was clear, distinct, without a flaw or an error, for over an hour. No human being could be capable of such oratory."

Misses S. A. and E. A. Arnott say :

" The greatest thing in our lives has happened that the Master showed himself. His face clearly shone forth, bright blue eyes, with reddish auburn beard and hair down to his shoulders. The light that shone from him was more than our eyes could stand. Then we got accustomed to the brilliant light and could watch every movement. It was a thrilling experience we will never forget. His words were perfectly formed and not a pause or a mistake did He make for over an hour. It was this that amazed us most. The form of the Doctor grew a few inches as the Master overshadowed him. This was the first experience we ever had in transfiguration, although we had heard much about it."

Mr. A. Thomas states :

" I am a most practical and critical person, being an engineer. I was always doubtful about what others saw and heard, and although I have read much on the subject of mediumship I was not convinced. But when I saw with my own eyes a light so bright that I had to close them, for it was some time before I could accustom my sight to the brilliance, then to see the face that is so familiar in many pictures of the Master, I was convinced that it was true. The Master's voice and speech were more than perfect. It is doubtful if any human being could perform such oratory.

" Although the Doctor is a good speaker I know he could not perform such a feat. My wife and her mother attended these talks and they also saw and heard the same as I did."

All present have testified in one way or another to the wonderful experiences they had during these talks by the Master.

TALK 1

I AM THE RESURRECTION AND THE LIFE—THE LOVE OF
GOD

> I am myself resurrection and Life, he who believes in me will
> live even if he dies, and no one who lives and believes in me
> will ever die.

1. God is Love and Love is God, yet no one knows what
It is—we only know that It *is*. Perhaps you have been
theorising—never do this! You must let the Truth unfold without suggestions from outside, and you must not
come to a conclusion, for this closes the avenue to Truth.

2. Love is the centre of the whole Universe, and from
this centre a continuous flow of Love flows through every
soul and through every thing that lives. Through flowers,
through animals, through human beings and angels, this
same Love flows continuously from its Central Font,
forever expressing Itself in Its true nature.

3. Love is the affinity in the minerals; Love is the
essence in the flowers; Love is expressed in the animal
nature. In man Love is expressed in affection, and, when
fully realised, the whole being is filled with It and every
cell in the body becomes vitalised.

4. There is no other power in the world but Love; It
is the only true Power in heaven and on earth, for It is
eternal and ever-present everywhere. The outer will pass
away, but Love shall forever be, for it is the Omnipresence
of God.

5. Theorising on Love is but a mental aspect of It. To
theorise on what Love is, is to lose its power. You are the
creation of the Infinite Life which is Love, and Love
expresses Itself in Its true nature when understood and
realised in this way.

6. All great souls upon the earth are expressing this Love in different ways in different parts of the world.

7. Suggestions come from outside—but you cannot understand the Truth from suggestions that arise from outside yourselves. Therefore do not come to any conclusion in regard to the Truth, for the Truth is unfathomable and eternal. I am ever-present, expressing myself in my Divine nature which is Eternal.

8. You must accept this, yet you must not come to conclusions of what It is, or what It is not.

9. Remember, this mighty power is waiting to unfold in you ; you are the vehicle prepared by It ; your soul is the vehicle through which It will flow. To be conscious of this is the secret of the God-man.

10. What is space ? You are now learning the rapidity of thought transference which is between you and the mind which is influencing you. These thoughts know nothing of distance.

11. Nathaniel asked, " Whence do you know me ? " " Even before Philip called you, while you were under the fig tree I saw you. Truly, I say to all of you that from now on you will see the heavens opened and the Angels of God ascending and descending to the Son of Man."

12. You have already witnessed this Truth. All are angels in the making ; you are born angels, the angelic birth exists in you. This is the Love of God. Some angels, now existing, are those who once lived on one planet or another.

13. The whole Universe is one complete whole, expressing the Divine Nature of Love. Love is the holy cohesive quality, the only power that can sustain all things, and is bringing about Its own perfection.

14. There is never anything wrong where Love exists, for It is complete in Itself.

15. There is nothing that can interfere with the current

of pure thought directed from Life, for really there is no distance ; the only necessity is a condition of receptivity.

16. It is now possible to receive this wonderful gift of the Father that is being poured out eternally. You can experience It for yourselves by opening yourselves up to It. You do not receive It from the external, only know that It is eagerly waiting to express Itself from the very centre of your being.

17. You must become consciously aware of It, and, when you are consciously aware of It, then you will experience It in every cell of your body, in your surroundings, in your friends, in your business place, your home— all can be filled with It. And there is nothing that can withstand It. It is so solid in Its nature that It interpenetrates every single particle of substance that exists in the Universe. It supports the whole Universe, and It gives breath and life ; " I am the Life and Love."

18. All your thoughts of Love and Healing sent out even without any special direction are caught up in the stream, and they help all. Remember nothing is lost in this world of thought charged with Love.

19. Space is a wrong idea ; it belongs to separation, but in Reality there is no separation.

20. Let your hearts and minds rest undisturbed in the realisation of the omnipresence of God. Even the child will come to know that there is no space or distance, for you all dwell in God and there is absolutely nothing outside God.

21. By my own experiences I found that the flesh changes through the conscious awareness of the Divine Essence of Love. It is the Power that creates all things and attracts everything to It.

22. For God who made the world and all things therein, and Who is the Lord of Heaven and Earth, does not dwell in temples made with hands, neither is ministered unto by

human hands, nor is He in need of anything, for it is He who gave Life and breath to all men.

23. And He has made of one blood all nations for to dwell on the face of the earth, so that they should seek and search after God and find Him by means of His Love and His Creations.

24. He is not far from any one of you. For in Him all live and move and have their being, and, as some of your wise men have said, " all are His kindred." Yes, when you have seen me you have seen the Father.

25. There is no mystery about these words when you thoroughly understand them. The mystery disappears when they are understood.

26. There cannot be one particle of substance that is not of God. Every particle in the whole Universe must be of God, for it is God alone who is expressing Himself, and I and the Father are one, there is no separation between us.

27. Now therefore, man, being of the family of God, is not bound to worship resemblances made of gold or silver or stone shapen by the skill and knowledge of man into resemblances of the Deity. Yet when men heard of the resurrection of the dead they mocked.

28. Understand that the great Truth of the Omnipresence, the Omnipotence and the Omniscience of God is complete. Know that it is He Who lives, and He alone lives, in every living thing because He created all of them and He could not live apart from His creations, for He is omnipresent.

29. If His creations were in any way separated from Him He could not be Infinite in nature, He could not be complete in Himself. Every creation was created with the fundamental principle of Love harmonising every action, bringing into manifestation His Divine nature. And when man becomes aware of this Truth, then shall man create

in himself the reflection of that perfect Divinity which will bring about his Heaven on earth.

30. And they mocked because they heard of the resurrection of the dead. Yet how could there be anything dead in the living Universe ? How could there be anything dead in the Eternal Living God ? Admitted there is change taking place everywhere, but there is nothing dead in that change ; every particle is a living particle which changes from one form to another. What ignorant man sees is death, what enlightened man sees is the action of Life. Ignorant man does not understand the law of transition from the one state to another, therefore man creates in his own mind the illusion he calls death.

31. Not one particle of the whole Universe is dead ; every particle is alive, existing in God. Every particle, even in its process of change, is a living expression of Life. And the fundamental principle under it all is the power of Love flowing from the Central Font of Love to Its smallest creations.

32. Your sense-mind would cloud or hide the vision, the vision of the completeness of that which is Divine in nature.

33. But now you are in the secret place of the most High, and He shall wipe away all tears from your eyes, and there shall be no more death, neither shall there be any more pain, for the former things pass away.

34. " I am Alpha and Omega, the beginning and the end ; I will give freely of the fountain of living water to him who is athirst. I am in myself the beginning and the end, I am He whom the prophets have spoken of, I am the Lord, the Christ that dwells in each and every one of you, and there is no separation between us, yet you have placed me so far away beyond your reach."

35. In your own minds you have thought me unattainable, yet I am living in the secret chambers of your hearts urging you continuously to recognise me.

36. This is the Christ that is born in the human family, the Christ that is born in every babe. It is the Christ that is eternal and lives after so-called death. It is the Christ in you that shall live forever.

37. Even as the rivers flow out and refresh the earth, so can you release that stream of Eternal Life into the outer. The unseen Spiritual Substance is alone substantial and is the only Reality that can be expressed in your personal life now.

38. Your consciousness is the reflection of It, your consciousness in the material or physical is the reflection of this Eternal Life expressing Itself, and as you become more aware of It, It becomes more real to you.

39. The brain, the nervous system, and the flesh of the body become filled with It. It raises the vibration of your mind to a state beyond your earthly existence. Yes, in time It will transform the body to make it that perfect instrument, for the Divine in nature is the only Reality.

40. Use every opportunity to express that which you know. Let your Love flow out and bless every brother, every sister, so that all your divisions will be swept away by the ocean of Love welling up in human hearts and lives. When you bless a brother and a sister with this love, in and out of your own being flows the Christ Life and Love.

41. Do not in any way disregard the truths that are written in the New Testament. If you express that which is true, you will also become true. Your true nature is Divine, let this nature become yours now, because now is Eternity, every moment of Life is *now*. Therefore remember not the past nor be anxious for the future; the future is taken care of, by your living now.

42. You must all come to the understanding of the Omnipresence that fills all space, knows nothing of past

or future but is eternally present, the same yesterday, to day and forever.

43. When you begin to know that all time is the present, you cease to " long," you cease to long for things to come, and a great strain drops from you. How many of you are straining to-day ? Because you are not living in the Omnipresence that is omnipresent. You live in a past and a future and miss the glorious expression of the Divine Life now.

44. Peace will come into your souls, things that troubled you before will no longer beset you. You will not be burdened with the things of the world because you will know that all that is mine is thine.

45. Spirit is all power, and directs all things, but if you stand on the outside looking in, then there is no possibility of your ever partaking of the feast spread before you : but if you will come inside, you can partake of the feast now and there will never be any other time but now.

46. When you gain this understanding, you eager souls—who feel that you must accomplish so much in a given time—will come to know that Love and service are pleasure and rest.

47. These words seem strange to you at first because you do not understand them. To rest in the Lord means to be always with the Lord ; and as the Lord is the supreme expression of the Almighty, knowing this, there is no fear, there is no doubt, and Life becomes a joy.

48. Only when you are burdened with the cares of the world is there sorrow. Lift up your hearts and rejoice in the fact that your Father knoweth what you are in need of and has prepared everything for you ; the table is already set. You can come into the feast now if you will, and partake of all that you are capable of ; the only thing that is necessary is your capacity to receive.

49. You will renew your energies and unfold wider

avenues for further experience, with a sense of peace and
quiet that comes from that which does not consider time
or space as an essential factor, for It knows no time or
space, being Ever-present and Eternal.

50. To live in the spiritual is to live in Reality, not
spasmodically and in limits. How can there be any time
or space in Infinity? Know that you live in the Mind of
God that fills all space, for there is nowhere where It is
not.

51. If you truly know that you are the Christ of God
that exists eternally and is ever-present, the animating
and Creative Power within the Mind, then there can be no
time or space.

52. You can reach the state where there is no time or
space and enter into the completeness of the Lord thy
God, that dwells in your soul ; the Lord is the only Power
there is. *I am* the Lord.

53. " Love " is the eternal ever-present and glorious
Life now, which is a rest and a joy, a satisfaction too full
to make you look backward or forward when you know
that Love is the ever-present Life now. The soul who has
realised this moves in the sufficiency of the Presence, that
is ever active in the present and never in the past or the
future.

54. Think over this carefully, so that your joy may be
full. " I am " the ever-present Love. It was this Love
that I saw so clearly. I knew that God was Love, and to
be His son then I must be Love also. I found there could
be nothing else for me but Love, and no matter what was
done to me I still knew that I must remain the son of
God, the Eternal Ever-present perfect LOVE that knew
no past or future, no sin or death.

55. " Lazarus come forth," was to speak from the
Spiritual plane, realising only the ever-present Life. If
you can understand these words, you will realise the Life

that is eternal and ever-present. You can also speak the word, if your consciousness can grasp the Reality of It, and what you speak shall manifest because it is created in the *now*.

56. You are affected by suggestions that come from without, suggested to by the conditions surrounding you ; you believe in death and decay ; but in Reality there is no death nor decay, there is only change, and this is Life. If you could see this ever-present Life behind all change and become consciously aware of It, then I say that every particle of your whole body would be filled with It.

57. " I am " the Lord, " I " change not. Open your eyes and see within yourselves this mighty Truth.

58. You can be just as much of God as you are prepared to manifest. Christ, the Son of God, in the heart of humanity reaches out to man urging him to awaken to his Divine Consciousness, for the Christ in each and every one is alive forever. There is eternal peace in the heart as you recognise this Truth.

59. " I am the Lord thy God. I am one with the Father, the Father and I are never apart, we are always working together in you."

60. The seven acts of Christ become actual to you now, at this moment, instead of belonging to a past period. The Christ experiences the birth of Life in the Temple that is not made with hands.

61. The symbol of the Divine child in the arms of Mary, the Mother, is but the symbol of the Christ being born in every babe. The Father is individualised in each and every one, thus manifesting the birth of Christ the Eternal Son of God into earthly Life.

62. Look around you and look at each other and say, " From whence didst thou come ? " Only the Father knoweth.

63. The anointing is the consecration of the life to God. Then cometh the awakening of the Christ in the Temple that is made by God alone.

64. According to your realisation the Christ manifests in you, so do you consecrate your life to God.

65. Then comes the temptation. Temptation was in the world for the Christ to overcome : " I have overcome the world."

66. The crucifixion means that everyone is crucified. All must pass through their own gates of Gethsemane ; some pass through it one way, some another. Thus you are purified through your experience.

67. The greatest of all experiences was that I could lay down my life through the crucifixion to take it up again, not for my own benefit but for the benefit of all who live, " and those who believeth in me will never die," for they have already found the secret of Eternal Life.

68. Then comes the resurrection, the resurrection of the soul out of this mortal body. The Christ is the Spirit of God manifesting in the flesh, the ascension is the true recognition of this Reality, the true realisation of the Eternal Christ.

69. The Christ is in you and nothing can avail from without ; the evolution of the one Soul exalts the whole race, that they may all be one.

70. The complete understanding of time as the only present factor, with neither past nor future, would remove false ideas and inherited ills. Only the good that man does has any vitality. Then cease to uphold the working-out of ignorance and sin, and things of the past.

71. Most people's minds are overburdened with the power of sin. The ignorance in the world and the sin in the world are all they can see. You cannot see the Christ through ignorance and sin. You can only see Christ through the Love of God ; the complete and perfect

expression of the Father of Love is His Son who lives forever in the present.

72. I am the son of God through Love. So also must you become the sons and daughters of God through Love. In no other way can you become true sons and daughters of God.

73. You are born sons and daughters of God because the Christ the Spirit of God is in you. When Christ is realised you will know yourself to be. Then the flood of Love flows through the heart that understands ; this is beyond the conception of any human soul that has not yet awakened.

74. In your physical sense you make both good and evil seem of equal power. This is but theorising with mortal sense, it is not the truth of Reality.

75. In God there is neither good nor evil, God is the complete perfect expression now. If you say that the omnipresent God is good and that evil exists also, then your reason is at fault—how can evil exist in the omnipresent good ?

76. Your misconceptions cause you to believe that evil exists. Do not theorise, but allow the Love of God to express Itself through you ; and you will find that which makes you fear, that which hinders your true expression, will dissolve away into nothingness—where it belongs. Think, and you will see that it is in your own mind that you are creating fear and evil, for it does not and cannot exist in the omnipresence of God.

77. Love is the only reality and is ever-present ; then realise that this Ever-present is Eternity free from all conditions.

78. Darkness is but the absence of light. When your hearts are full of Love there can be no darkness in the soul, for Love is the Light of the world. Truth is the search for the Light of the world ; " Love " is the first

Cause, and when you find this truth you have found everything. As Love casteth out fear, so does Love cast out all that is contrary to the true nature.

79. Fear is a thought-power generated by the self through lack of understanding and has the temporary effect of interrupting the flow of Life through the soul and body.

80. Would you fear if you knew that *you* were the Lord ? Would you fear if you knew that the Christ was *your* real self ? Would you fear if you knew that God alone existed and it was He who was expressing Himself, and that *you*, His creation, could never be separated from Him ?

81. Look to the Cross and see what lesson it brings you. Would you deny the Father, even though you were scourged and crucified with nails through hands and feet ? Your only strength lies in Him who is with you always, who created you like unto Himself—LOVE.

82. Fear has the effect of changing the body through chemicalisation, but to overcome these conditions you apply the antidote of Love, the only permanent power in the Universe.

83. Every thought, every movement, every action has a chemical change upon the body. You are continuously changing your body structure through fear and anxiety ; this is inharmony. But Love is harmony and healing for soul and body.

84. Love is the power that overcomes all things and is working through all Nature. God is expressing Himself, sustaining the body, the temple not made with hands.

85. When you let go of your fears you will find that your God-nature will bring back the normal state of the body, which is harmony.

86. Nothing has been brought into being except through the Christ. As John said, the Word was with God and the Word was God, and the Word was made flesh ; and only

through that Word did everything come into being. I am that Word, I am the Word of God, I am the Life, I am the Lord.

87. See clearly this Truth in yourselves, knowing that which is possible to me is also possible to you if you will believe in me.

88. Peace and calm will come into your hearts when you know that you are passing through all stages of the Christ from the birth to the Ascension.

89. Love is power and Life's true expression. Love pours forth from its fountain in one continuous stream and is the only power there really is.

90. Love is the Life Energy passing through the body. Love is a passion of great power in the heart. Love is the protective agency in every living soul. Love flows though all planes of being ; Love is the foundation of all Divine action and is the salvation of the Race.

91. When you realise that this Love is within yourselves, then the mighty Power grows from within you. No power comes from without.

92. Love pours forth from its Source in one continuous stream and is the only Real Power there is ; the soul and body are sustained by It.

93. It is the rapture in the heart, the protector of the soul and body. All Divine action is based upon the Love of God.

94. All are subject to the Divine ; the more you know this, the more like God you become. All are subject to the same power, for there is no other Power but the Power of the Infinite Living Life. Therefore the omnipresence of His Divine Nature is a Reality.

95. Love is the only Power that exists in the whole Universe : everything responds to it. Flowers, animals, humans and Angels all respond to Love's adoration.

96. Love being God, It must be the greatest power there

is. Love harmonises everything. Love cannot be separate from anything in Nature, for It is the cause behind all true manifestation, and will remain when all other conditions are removed.

97. Do not think that the Father has left you when you find yourself in distress. He is making you more perfect, a more perfect instrument through which He can manifest His Creative Power.

98. Ignorance has no principle in itself, just as error has no principle. Mathematics has a principle, but error can have none, for when the error is corrected it disappears ; therefore you learn that ignorance and error have no power of their own.

99. The prophet wrote in Proverbs, " My son, eat this honey because it is good, and this honeycomb which is sweet to thy taste ; so shall the knowledge of wisdom be unto thy soul, when thou hast found it ; then there shalt be reward and thy expectations shall not be cut off."

100. Love is the secret balm that all can use, the learned and the untutored, the wise and the foolish. It speaks all languages, and It is the soul's haven of rest.

101. The position you hold in the world means nothing. What means most to you is your capacity to receive and give Divine Love, the true expression of God Himself.

102. God is Spirit, and Spirit is Life ; Life is Love ; and Love is the vital force in all things ; It is the harmony in all things ; then we must worship in Love if we would attain a consciousness of God.

103. Idols and images are but symbols in the mind and we gain little from them ; we must realise the Love of God. Christ is the Spirit of God, and has been given all power in heaven and on earth through Love.

104. People are mystified by the healings that took place 2,000 years ago, but there is very little difference in the healings that take place in your midst to-day ; the

only difference is the fact that it may be a different personality used. But it is the same Christ that heals.

105. The Real is the Principle of Love. God made the Universe by pure thought, positive and creative, which is the expression of His nature " Love." Then Love is the union between God and mankind. This Divine Energy is the eternal link that holds us fast to Him who made us in His own image and likeness.

106. So mankind becomes the vehicle for the expression of Love, and this is the true science of Living.

107. As we gaze upon the Fountain of Love, God's nature becomes our nature. What I see the Father do, I do likewise. It is no longer strange to you now, that my thoughts become the healing power that changes the ether of disease and death to those of Health and Life.

108. By the power of the holy thought your bodies will also be changed from carnal flesh to spirit form.

109. All are sons and daughters of God by birth, and all become sons and daughters of God through understanding and Love. There is nothing so great in the heart of man as the expression of his Christ nature : there is no greater power in all the world. *By Love I heal, by Love I live.*

110. Through true understanding the truth is revealed —that we are all sons and daughters of God ; and from this point alone you become a greater civilisation upon earth.

111. The Love of God through the Christ must dwell in each and every one of you. Seek ye first the Kingdom of God and His righteousness, and everything else shall be added unto you.

112. And when you pray, believe you have received that which you have asked for, and ye shall have it. When you ask, ask in the Mind of God ; it is then established in the Spirit, and what is established in the Spirit must come forth in form, provided you make yourself receptive to it through understanding Faith.

113. You shall all gain your inheritance even in the darkness that surrounds you, for the Light that lighteth the world is within yourselves and can never be extinguished.

114. We are all joint heirs to all that is God's when we attain to an understanding heart full of Love. " Son thou art ever with me, all that is mine is thine."

115. Through my lips, to unawakened earth comes the Trumpet of Truth. The Lord thy God is one Lord, and this is the Infinite Spirit within all mankind.

116. I am the Light of the world ; he who follows me will never walk in darkness ; he will enjoy the light of Life.

117. The Pharisees said, " You are testifying to yourself ; your evidence is not valid." Is it not the same to-day ?

118. I replied to them, " Though I do testify to myself, my evidence is valid, because I know where I have come from, and where I am going to—whereas you do not know where I have come from, or where I am going to. You judge by the outside. I judge no one ; and though I do judge, my judgment is true, because I am not by myself—there is myself and the Father who sent me."

PEACE AND LOVE BE WITH YOU

O Eternal Father of Love, we rejoice in Thy Presence. We know Thou art with us always, and we can never be apart from Thee. We are expressing Thy Life and Love. Thou didst send me into this world to prepare others for that which is to come. And they shall become Thy Angels to administer to others Thy Love. This is the joy of Life ; let this joy be theirs, as it is mine for ever and ever. Make it their watchword in the morning, noon and night, so that they shall always be at peace. Even if ignorance darkens the light of Thy Presence, help them to see the Divine Truth : " I am the Lord ; I have been given power and dominion over all things." Thy Peace I leave with them, for Thy peace is eternal, and as they seek it so shall they find it. AMEN.

(THE SCRIBE'S REMARKS :

This was the first talk to us by the Master. Those present were amazed beyond words, for most had never seen a transfiguration before. A shaft of light shone from above, lighting up the Auditorium, and the face of the Master was clearly seen, and those who witnessed it were different henceforth.)

TALK 2

" . . . And a Voice Came from Heaven "

1. These talks are being recorded as I speak ; this will help you to remember what I have said. It is difficult to remember all the words that are spoken, and it is difficult to convey to the mind the meaning behind the words, but if you will pay attention you will be able to understand. My words are profound, pregnant with the everlasting Truth.

2. The only way that you can convey to the mind something that is indescribable is by means of giving the key so that you can open the door yourselves, and this is the meaning of the words " . . . and a voice came from heaven."

3. Heaven is not a place but an awareness of God. What are you conscious of ? Think for a moment ! Are you just conscious of yourselves, conscious of things external, conscious of what you see and hear with your eyes and ears ? Or are you conscious of an inner voice which is waiting to reveal Itself to you, revealing Its greatness, Its mighty power in your lives ?

4. When we last gathered here together, I made it plain that the Infinite—the Life and Love I spoke to you about—is above and beyond the conception of the mortal sense, yet I know that God is Infinitely meek and lowly, as well as great and wondrous. He fills all space and creates all, and, as you become conscious of this all-pervading Life, It is the answer to the soul's deepest and highest aspirations, for Love fulfils Itself.

5. This Love is the only power existing in the world, and when you grasp this thoroughly you will no longer

fear. Love flows from the Central Font of the Infinite Himself, expressing Itself in everything from the very lowest to the highest. It flows through all planes of manifestation, from the mineral substance to the highest angelic Beings existing in the Cosmos.

6. Learn first and thoroughly that " you are " and will be for ever. Your present condition is an opportunity for Spiritual advancement. The condition in which you are in at the present time is one that is most necessary.

7. When you come to learn the great Truth that Spirit is all there is, and that there can be nothing but Spirit, the scales fall from your eyes.

8. I am obliged to use your words and modes of expression. These are wholly inadequate to convey Spiritual truths, yet, by opening yourselves to the Spirit within, you will know what I have said is true.

9. So we will consider together the great truths of God and mankind His offspring.

10. You, the real you, are not the outward or visible form, nor is your personality the real you, for this is far from the true likeness of your real self. You are a Conscious Being that lives in Reality, the voice from heaven. Become aware of this voice from heaven within, and you will know me also.

11. When you see a most beautiful scene and you wish to portray that scene on canvas, the result is but a copy of it and can never compare with the real. It is the same with you.

12. The real is in the Spiritual plane and exists there as your true self. The outer is but a copy, and is blurred by the artistry of the mind reacting to the external world through the senses.

13. Allow the real within to manifest in the outer, Its wondrous power of Love and Peace. The Creative Principle existing throughout the whole Universe is

invisible to the eyes of humans, invisible to the eyes of Angels, yet it exists as the only Reality in all, as the building process, the Creative Principle in everything, and through it all visible things must come. Then do not blur the outer through ignorance and fear.

14. I am the Life ! I know myself as Life ; therefore, in my knowing, I become the Life, and through me and by me everything has been made that is *made*. I and the Father are one, for there is no other Life.

15. I cannot convey in words to you what I see and know, yet within yourselves is the Spirit that will enlighten you of the glory that remains permanently " now " for you to realise.

16. The realisation of this Spiritual power was the basis of Peter's faith, and enabled my disciples to perform miracles—yet there is no miracle when the Law is understood. And when you also realise this mighty power within, you will know that the Creative Principle is in your own consciousness, your consciousness being the means through which It is expressed. Through your consciousness everything manifests in your own life, for it is the Father Himself who is living in you. This is what I am aware of always ; this is what you must also be aware of.

17. Children know things instinctively. Many pertinent questions that a child desires to know remain unanswered through the ignorance of those who are supposed to guide it. These questions remain unanswered for perhaps a lifetime before being asked again. The soul that desires the truth can open the Door, for : " Behold I stand at the door and knock, and whosoever opens I will come in and sup with him and he with me." This is the great mighty Truth of the Living God : I and the Father are one.

18. The realisation of this Truth enables that which is

ever-present to come forth in your own lives. There is a great force of Creative Power working in and through you—yet you do not see it. Yet It is that which in Itself manifests, and must do so through you, for you were specially made for that purpose.

19. I want you to think clearly on what I have said, so that you can realise the indescribable Truth that mortal mind cannot describe. The Indescribable can only be realised, for the Indescribable is in Itself the Truth, and will manifest completely when you realise It. It is not WHAT It is, but THAT It is.

20. You create anew by the Life that flows from the centre of all Life and Love. Thus the will of God is done on earth as it is done in heaven, and this can be done in you " now."

21. There seems to be a barrier between the visible and the invisible, that separates us, but this is not true ; there is no barrier except in your own minds, there alone exists the barrier between us. Then get rid of this barrier, this separation, through understanding and Love.

22. When you enter into the greater Consciousness of God you will no longer be content with the shadows of things but will seek that which is real and substantial. The invisible is the substantial, the visible is but the shadow.

23. When you see something through your mortal eyes, you say it is real because you can feel it and see it. What you are seeing is but the outer expression of something greater that remains invisible, the Creative Power, the Life, the only eternally existing power in the Universe, and this is the Life-Principle that lives in you and me and in every living thing. This Life is love, this Life is peace. " I am the Life."

24. You think that the passing of great minds from your midst is a loss ; this is not so, for these minds become

greater and have not left you. They live more in Reality than ever before.

25. Therefore you have not lost anything, but have gained a great deal more. Think of your own dear ones who have passed beyond the flesh ; you think you have lost them. I can assure you that is not true, they are greater now than they have ever been and they are nearer to you now than they have ever been.

26. You realise now that I have not left you, but am still with you. I am in the world transforming the world, uplifting the minds of all to see the Truth that dwells within, so that all people shall become aware of their Divine Nature.

27. The more you know of your true Self the more you will understand me.

28. The great mistake most make is to think that I and My disciples have sojourned to some far-off place, there to wait till some future date when you may arrive at the same place, if you get the passport from some organisation that claims to be able to get you an entry.

29. There is no place, only a state of consciousness ; and we are with you now. The more you realise this, the more we can come into your lives and help you.

30. Think of what the Consciousness of God means to you now. It is the same consciousness in me as it is in you. There is no difference in the consciousness ; the only difference is in the degree of awareness or the realisation of consciousness.

31. The Consciousness of God is not split up in parts ; you cannot say that you are a particle of this or a particle of that ; God is one whole, complete, expressing Himself, and you live and move and have your being in Him and He lives in you. Through your consciousness you become aware of this, and then your consciousness becomes the power over all things.

32. No earnest prayer is ever disregarded. God knows before you ask what you are in need of.

33. God is Love and you must reverence Him with your hearts full of love. What man is there of you, when if his son ask bread will give him a stone, or if he ask a fish will give him a serpent ?

34. If ye then, being ignorant of true Love, know how to give things unto your children, how much more shall your Father who is Real Love give good things to them that ask Him.

35. Some think God is afar off when they pray ; I say to you, go into your closet and close the door and there pray in secret, for your Father hears in secret, and He shall reward thee openly.

36. The meaning is quite plain. In your own secret chambers there dwells the Almighty. The Almighty is not afar distant from you but is the living expression of Reality in you, your Reality, your Real Self.

37. When you pray earnestly in this " knowing " in secret, in the quiet of your own soul, the whole Universe is brought into action to create and express that which you ask.

38. All real prayers are answered instantly, and the time will come when your prayers will also be answered instantly. You must practice praying, practice praying in *secret* with your mind at peace. Believe you have received, and you shall have.

39. It is wonderful to understand that we, you and I, and all others with us, are one great united unlimited whole, one family in which there is no separation, only Love.

40. Perhaps you cannot grasp this at first, but, as you open yourselves to the Spirit of Truth, the Comforter that is always with you will reveal all to you. " I am " the Comforter, " I am " the Life.

41. I am the Life, and he who believes in Me shall not die, and even if he were dead he shall live, because I am the Life in you. He who believeth in Me has everlasting Life ; therefore there can be no death, for I am ever alive in you.

42. It is the same Spirit in all. A drop of the ocean has the same quality as all the ocean. I am everywhere.

43. By understanding and love, so do you enter into the Christ that dwells in all souls, for there " I " abide.

44. Ye have heard what I said unto you, " I have set the Lord always before me because He is at my right hand and I shall not be moved."

45. How slowly do you truly learn that God and man are one. You are afraid to throw away your limitation, like children you cling to your toys, your walls, your partitions, your churches, your chapels, your synagogues, your mosques. Oh, could I gather you all together under my wings and show you the one Life in all !

46. You often wonder why you are so long in learning that God is all Life and that this Life is perfect Love— seen and unseen. This is because you try to grasp the truth from without, instead of from within.

47. How you all like to cling to the things that you are afraid to lose. He who retains his life will lose it ; he who gives up his life will retain it.

48. I speak from the Christ, I always did, and that is why my words seemed strange to those who live only in the outer. Millions are still in bondage, yet at all times my door is open to all, to come in and sup with me.

49. A Satan tries to bar the way, and that Satan is the false personality, the Satan of the senses, that all have to overcome.

50. This illusion of the mortal sense is the only hindrance to the realisation of true Spiritual Consciousness, for the Kingdom of Heaven is within yourselves. I am

the Life, the same of 2,000 years ago. As Moses and Elijah were 2,000 years before my appearance on earth yet it was the same Life expressed in all. I am before Abraham.

51. Time does not exist ; I am now as I was and always will be. In this realisation you must also remember that you are the living expression of the Almighty, for the Father is ever working in you.

52. The Divine Power that exists in you is the same as in me, and, as your consciousness unfolds into the greater Consciousness of God, so you will know me.

53. The Voice of the Christ is fearless and all-powerful. Christ is the conqueror, and will conquer, for it is the Law of God that the Christ shall have dominion over all things.

54. The symbol of the Cross is the Christ in man over-coming the world, the awakening in the Temple not made with hands, the consecration, the temptation, the crucifixion, the resurrection and the ascension. This is the Christ, the Conqueror. The stages I have already explained to you, and thus it will be unnecessary for me to explain again ; but, if you read my words again, the Spirit within you will reveal more of the Truth.

55. As you unfold, so will the Spirit reveal to your consciousness the secret that dwells within the secret chambers of your heart. I am the Life, I am the Truth, I am the Way, no one enters to the Father except through me—the Christ—there is no other way, there has never been any other way.

56. The Christ is the Word of God, the Word that was God, the Word that was with God, and the Word that was made flesh.

57. This is your real self, in Reality, as God the Father knows you, and so you must know yourself to be.

58. The voice of the carnal sense is the voice of the shadow, the Satan that suggests separation. limitation,

sickness, death. Then hold fast to the Christ, the only begotten son of God, the Father of all.

59. Do not fear Satan, for there is nothing to fear ; all you need say is, " Get thee behind me, Satan of the carnal mind. I am the Son of God, the Son of Man, I am the conqueror. I do not live by myself but the Father, who is always with me, He is my guide."

60. These things I have said to you, that in me you may have peace. In the world you will have tribulation but have courage, I have conquered the world, and so shall you conquer the world.

61. The Father, the overruling Spirit, the Living Life, the Christ is His Son, that dwells in every soul, and the Holy Ghost is the expression of the Christ Consciousness in wholeness, in the understanding of " I am the Life." Nothing can assail you, for I am the conqueror within. If you can feel this Truth in your own heart and mind you will know that you are also the conqueror, and you will know also that you are free. So you will overcome the Satan of the senses. " Get thee behind me, Satan."

62. Then worship God through Christ ; there is no other way, there never has been except in name. I am He who lives, was crucified, and behold I am alive forever more.

63. I am the Way, the Truth, and the Life ; no man comes to the Father except by me. Christ is the Consciousness of the Supreme Infinite Life manifesting in the world.

64. The Christ is the Truth, the Life, the Love, that unites all to God, and only through Love can you be with God, for God is Love.

65. I am one with the Father through Love. Thou shalt love the Lord thy God with all thy soul, with all thy heart, with all thy mind, with all thy strength, and thou shalt love thy neighbour as thyself.

66. Christ is the Son of God born into the world and he remains in the world till the world is transformed, so that the will of the Father which is done in Heaven shall also be done on earth.

67. The one title for God is " Our Father," and it is the best I know ; and it becomes more comprehensive as you grow into the knowledge of Him who created you.

68. You are His reflection, His likeness. When you know the Father and you are one, the union that always exists becomes known to you. But these words must not remain in your mind as mere words ; you must truly understand them. The true meaning of these words can only come from within yourselves.

69. What you are hearing now through your ears will remain with you. You will remember these words that I have spoken. They will linger in your hearts till the Spirit of Truth begins to manifest in you ; then you will know the true meaning of my words. That, that which is already established in the consciousness of God must be established in the consciousness of man. And through the realisation and the recognition of your oneness with the Father, so is this consciousness established in you.

70. I know how true this is. All those who have passed into the higher realms of consciousness begin to understand the mighty power that comes through this realisation.

71. This very form that I am overshadowing to-night is, as you see, youthful in expression, the face is filled with vitality, the body is filled with a force that regenerates every cell of the body. This is because my consciousness at the moment is one with his consciousness. The consciousness of our beloved brother is one and the same with mine at this moment as I overshadow him. In Reality there is no separation between us. Separation is a mental illusion.

72. Great is this mighty Truth ! If you can receive this influence now, every one of your bodies shall be charged with life, for the Father dwells in you too.

73. Everything has been entrusted to me by my Father, and no man knoweth who is the Son except the Father, and who is the Father except the Son and to whomsoever the Son wishes to reveal Him.

74. These words seem strange to you, but when you think deeply about them you will see the inner meaning.

75. The Father knows the Son and the Son knows the Father, and the Son can also reveal the Father to those to whom he wishes to reveal the, Father, because the Son knoweth the Father and the Father knoweth the Son.

76. Blessed are those who see what you see, and hear what you hear.

77. I have been given the power of victory, for the Son lives in the Father and the Father lives in the Son. How can mere words explain this truly glorious Truth ? Only by the Spirit that is within you, the Comforter that is always with you, ready waiting to express Himself, can this truth be known.

78. Ask and the gift will be yours. Seek and you will find, knock and the door will open to you, for everyone who asks receives, the seeker finds, the door is opened to anyone who knocks.

79. " Whatever you would have men do unto you, you do the same to them." Know, in your own heart, that which you see in others is established in yourselves, and whatsoever you would have man do unto you do first unto them.

80. Never be troubled about to-morrow : " now " is the only time, make NOW your reality and to-morrow will take care of itself. Then do not worry about the future and miss the wonderful NOW. The consciousness can only create in the now, not to-morrow ; not in the

yesterday, yesterday is but a memory, to-morrow is but a hope ; now is the only creative moment.

81. You can only create in the mind of God moment by moment and that is now, and that which you create in the mind of God now is already established ; then to-morrow takes care of itself.

82. Do not weep with those who weep, but help them by the mighty Love that reigns within ; as a mother would love her child so must you feel that Love for all. All are the children of God, from the highest to the lowest, and when you recognise this you will know only one family where there is no separation.

83. Learn to become unselfish ; this is the secret of receptivity. You are not a bit of Spirit but you are one with the whole. Spirit cannot be separated from Itself.

84. When you truly become aware of this, transformation takes place, for receptivity is to receive. The Truth is that God is always pouring His gifts out to all, and if you want His gifts you have to open up to receive. This receptivity is the secret of greatness ; the secret of all true existence is unselfishness. Therefore giving is receiving.

85. I often wonder what your thought would be if you could see what I see at this moment—thousands upon thousands now listening to these words, bringing clearer the understanding that the Love of God dwells on earth as it does in heaven, dwells in the outer as it does in the inner.

86. I have said, " If you know me, you will know my Father too, but if you do not know my Father, how can you know me, or understand my word ? "

87. I speak from the Christ—where do you speak from ? The mortal sense ? Do you react to conditions or do you realise that within yourselves dwells the Power of God, the consciousness of " I am the Life," " I am the Truth," " having dominion over all things " ?

88. Within yourselves is the Father. Know that it is so and He will come forth through you. This is the Light of the World and the World does not overcome the Light but the Light overcomes the darkness. "I am" the Light of the World, and the darkness disappears because of my light.

89. This is the Light of man. It is the expression of Infinite Love and Wisdom and creates the perfect state in mankind.

90. The source of your being is God, and when you become awakened to this, you will know the Father Who is in the Son Who is in you also.

91. As the consciousness of the mortal sense becomes aware of the Christ consciousness the mortal sense is risen into the Christ consciousness. As the Christ, I overcame the world and all that is in the world ; I overcame mortal sense, the carnal mind, the satan of the senses, so shall you ; thus you will understand the voice from heaven is the consciousness of God.

92. Man by his own thoughts creates his prison walls. According to his concepts, so is he limited ; even your greatest conception is a limitation. It is not WHAT Life is but THAT Life is.

93. Creation on the plane of the concrete is the effect of the invisible Cause within. Your physical body serves as a starting point for further advancement, which has to be made through conscious realisation of the totality of all Spirit as the ever-present eternal and the only substance, power, Life ; Its expression being Love.

94. Love thy God with all thy heart, with all thy soul, with all thy mind, and love your neighbour as yourself. This is the Law upon which the foundation of the race stands.

95. In the parable of the prodigal Son is shown the Love of the Father ; the son's indulgence, his repentance, his regaining of himself—his true spiritual state. First of

all he suffers trials and tribulations, spends his inheritance, then he returns willingly to become a servant, yet becomes the Son as he always was the son.

96. The Father's Love is so great that, no matter what the son has done, the Father's love obliterates all error. How true this is in every life. Errors are corrected when you become aware of the Truth. It is experience through which you can rise out of conditions into the understanding of yourself. Then the error dissolves into nothingness, and the Truth stands free as It was from the beginning.

97. Repentance comes before forgiveness ; repentance comes from the heart of man as he realises the Father's Love, and he is forgiven. Then man regains his true Spiritual state, the awareness of himself in God, willing to become the servant of all, to do unto others as he would have others do unto him. It is when you become like the Prodigal Son that the feast is laid before you ; come in, partake of it now with Love for your brothers and sisters. For only through Love can you partake of the feast that the Father has prepared for you.

98. This is what you also have to learn upon earth. How often have you withheld your love from someone who you thought did wrong ? It is none of your business anyhow. It is all between the Father and His child, and, if you remember this, you will refrain from criticising others and turn this weapon upon yourselves first.

99. You will understand others better, when you see your own faults first.

100. You would condemn ! Condemn not, lest ye be condemned. Judge not, lest ye be judged. Take the plank out of your own eye, then you may be able to see better how to take the splinter out of your brother's eye.

101. We are finding channels everywhere, teaching all over the world by secret ways, as we are doing here. Not only are we teaching here in the physical plane, but also

in the inner planes, where some have not yet recognised
the true nature of their Being.

102. I am speaking not only to you but also to others
whom you do not see with mortal eyes.   When they
understand they will go forward to the glory that awaits
them. As they lift their consciousness into the higher state
they find that they are no longer bound to earth but are
free, released from the bondage they themselves created
in their own minds. Accept my word and you will also be free.

103. Keep your hearts full of Love to God and to all
mankind, and I will teach you much.

104. If you do not understand all that I say, wait,
listen, tune-in to me, for I am simple and easy to reach.

105. It is written in the prophets that the people shall
be all taught of God ; every man, therefore, that hath
heard, that hath learned of the Father, cometh unto me.

106. God who commanded the light to shine in the
darkness hath shone within my heart to give the light and
understanding of the glory of God.

PEACE AND LOVE BE WITH YOU

O Eternal Father, Thy Nature is planted in us all ; we
have realised Thy Presence and find Thy Nature expressing
Itself in our lives, blessing all and bringing all to Thee.
Loving Father, as Thy Son speaks, bless those who listen
to, and those who may read, Thy words with Love and
understanding.   Amen.

(THE SCRIBE'S REMARKS :

The written words, although inspiring and instructive,
miss the great Presence that gave an unforgettable
experience to those who listened to the words that fell
from his lips like pearls of great price. Yet they can be
pearls of great price to all who read this with understanding and Love.)

TALK 3

CHRIST IS THE LIFE IN YOU

1. The voice of the Christ is far-reaching. It reaches far and near, for It is the Omnipresence. Wherever the Father is, so am I ; and wherever I am, the Father is always with me.

2. The great Truth is that the Almighty God is all there is, and there is nothing existing except by Him and through His Son the Christ.

3. The peace of the world dwells in the Christ, waiting for every human soul to recognise the Christ Life, to manifest the love, beauty, strength, wisdom, and power of the Father.

4. There is peace and love abiding in each and every one of you, if you will only allow it to express itself through the recognition and realisation of this Truth, that the Father alone liveth and He is Love, Wisdom and Peace and the only Reality.

5. The Power of the Christ is developed in you through first recognition, then realisation, followed by periods of quiet to become more aware of the presence of the Lord thy God.

6. To realise the Truth is to know that *It is*. " I and the Father are one," the Father is greater than I, yet we work together as one. Without Him I can do nothing, but with Him I can do all the Father does, because we are one.

7. Recognition must come first, followed by realisation and periods of quiet, so that My power will be developed in your own consciousness. Yet there is only one Consciousness manifesting throughout the whole Universe,

that is the Consciousness that is in Life Itself. Life created all forms in which It can consciously manifest Its glory.

8. Life created the human soul and body so that Life could manifest in Its own awareness. When you truly know this, you bring into operation the Christ Power in your own life.

9. You must come out from your material or business life to rest awhile in the Kingdom of God, knowing that you are steadily growing and unfolding the true Life and Power of the Christ that waits to manifest in your life always.

10. Wait in silence, holding the attitude of the true expression of the Christ, and what It means to you. In this way steady growth is obtained.

11. This state is not one of " blankness," nor a state of " nothingness " as is advised by some ; neither is it one of strain in trying to force acceptance upon the consciousness without understanding.

12. You must avoid these extremes. Hold in your heart a stillness that is alive with true understanding, that there can be no separation between you and the Father.

13. Say in your heart : It is the Father who ever remains in me, He is doing the work. This unites your individual consciousness with your God Consciousness which is omnipresent.

14. I will express myself in my own true nature when you recognise me and the eternal aliveness of my Life. The recognition of the Eternal quality of my Life is the Christ manifesting in you. There is no greater power in heaven or on earth. All power has been given unto me in heaven and on earth. This is my true state, the manifestation of the Love of God. Think in your own hearts what this can be to you, with the aliveness of my living Presence always with you. In this realisation there is glory and peace.

15. Those who have passed beyond the physical body are still living. Some think they have not left the physical flesh, some are still dreaming ; but all will awaken to the truth of the living God, eternally expressing Himself in all. His expression is eternal and ever-present and is unfolding the Christ in you.

16. In this way the result will be most beneficial to yourself and all those whom you come into contact with. For the Christ—the God-power within—will assert Itself, and all discord will quietly dissolve away, for discord has no longer any power over you, except through your belief in it.

17. In your thought you think of me as quite different from yourselves. When you read in the Scriptures a history of what happened 2,000 years ago, you think I am of the past, yet I am ever-present with you. Remember that the same Spirit of God dwells in each and every soul, and he or she who does the Will of my Father is my mother, my sister, my brother.

18. It is the same Spirit of God that lives in me, lives in you. The same Christ shall manifest in you also through your recognition and realisation of this Truth, for you have also been given dominion over all things, and He who believeth in me shall do even greater things.

19. " I am " the innermost Spirit-Consciousness ; the Consciousness of the Christ is the Consciousness of God, the Father manifesting in the son.

20. Try to hold this truth so that it will reveal its power in your personal life. Become aware that you are conscious, that you are living ; your living, then, is the most dominant and important factor in your personal life.

21. Have you ever thought that your living is eternal, that you are life Itself, that you cannot live apart from Life ? Your consciousness is the means through which Life manifests Itself in the body, neither does the body

live apart from Life. Consciousness is in Life Itself and is the directing power within. " I am the Life."

22. Through the individual this power will manifest ; then know that all outside energy is a hindrance. The Christ is ever active and is never static. Christ is the creative energy with constant activity from within, the silence that is ever active, the Father who is ever doing the work. As you quietly wait upon Him, His breath renews every particle of your body by Its silent orderly activity.

23. My message is " I am the Life." You and me before God are the same. God's Spirit made me, and His almighty power resides in me, and the same Spirit remains in you.

24. I did not come to proclaim my own Divinity separate from humanity, but to show that I was in humanity and that all humanity is in me, and through the understanding of my words everyone will claim the Christ as the Saviour of the Race.

25. The Christ of God is the living Presence of God in each and every one of us—the Father manifesting Himself, and there can be no other, for He alone exists. He alone liveth as it was in the beginning, so it will always be. The Christ is not separate, the Christ is the same in you and in me. The Christ is the Father living, expressing Himself ; that is why I say, " I am the Life." The Father hath Life in Himself and grants the Son to have the same Life in himself.

26. " I " being the son of God occupy the place in the Creative Scheme I know I occupy, and the thing asked in its process of creation occupies a corresponding place, for I have proved that I have dominion over all things, and this you can also prove for yourselves if you will believe in me, and act on my words.

27. John said the word was in the beginning and that

very word was with God, and God was that word. The same was in the beginning with God.

Everything came to be by His hand, and without Him not even one thing came to be what was created.

The Life was in him, and the Life is the Light of man.

And the same Light shines in the darkness and the darkness does not overcome it.

He was the true Light which lighteth every man who came into the world.

He was in the world and the world was under his hand and yet the world knew him not.

He came unto his own and his own did not receive him. But those who believed in *his name* became the sons of God.

These are those who knoweth that they are not of blood, nor the will of the flesh, nor the will of man, but born of God the Father, and this word became flesh and dwelt amongst us.

28. This is the true interpretation of John's words given in the Aramaic language as written at that time. So we see how clearly it is shown that those who knoweth that they are not of blood nor of the will of the flesh but born of God the Father have Eternal Life now. God made things by becoming the things He made. The darkness did not overcome the light of man, for this light is the light that lighteth every soul that cometh into this world. The light exists in all humanity, for it was in humanity from the beginning ; this Light in man is the Christ of God.

29. This is the Word that dwells in every living soul. Truly I say unto you that every babe that is born, is born by the Word of God, and that Word is Christ that lives eternally. The flesh has no say in the matter.

30. Each individual makes the future by the thoughts and acts in the present, and " now " is always the present. In the " now " only can you create ; you cannot create in the future, nor can you create in the past.

31. The Christ is the Creative Power, and by that Power alone do all things come into being. When this realisation is strong in your consciousness, there is a freedom beyond the understanding of the human mind.

32. The mortal consciousness cannot understand the glory of this Truth, but through realisation your mortal consciousness will be lifted into the Consciousness of the Christ.

33. Hold the attitude in all you undertake that God never fails, that it is the Father who worketh in you. In this realisation all is possible to you. By yourself you are nothing, but with God you are everything ; say " I and the Father are one."

34. This attitude, which is the only true and substantial one, holds you above the mortal plane and you function in the Real—the Christ Consciousness. You are lifted out of the mortal sense, and henceforth all things are different.

35. Are you aware only of the things that surround you on the outside ? If you are, then you are still dwelling in the mortal sense. But I told you, the only true understanding is that the Spirit of God is manifesting through your consciousness, and this comes from within and not from without.

36. The Christhood of man is already complete. The Christ is the impersonal unselfish expression of a loving God in you and loving all, for all is God. The race must enter into this unity with Me.

37. This is the evolution of the outer, of which the inner is the Cause, ever urging onward and upward the true expression of that which is within. And the outer must become as the inner, and the inner shall become the outer.

38. The time will come when the glory of the Christ shall manifest completely in the flesh, for the flesh has no say in the matter. It is the decree of the Almighty that the Christ is supreme, and shall rule supreme. The Spirit in man is " I who liveth forever."

39. Christ is God and God is Christ. Rejoice that you have this this knowledge that the Christ of God worketh in you " now."

40. Live in the realisation of this Truth, so that the truth shall manifest in your life. Christ, the " Conqueror," will make you *free*.

41. Those who believe in the Christ are born of God and not of any impulse of flesh or of man. Call no one your Father upon earth, for one is your Father which is in heaven.

42. Perhaps you have not quite grasped the meaning of this saying. You are born in the flesh, but the flesh has no say in the matter. You are born of the Spirit, and the Spirit is the only creative power creating all things; this is the word that was with God, the word that was God, the word that was made flesh is immortal.

43. No one has ever seen God, but God has been un-folded by the Christ in me, and whoever sees me sees the Father.

44. God does not separate Himself ; He creates within Himself the likeness of Himself, and this is the Light in all mankind.

45. We are all of the same Life, for Life in Itself cannot be different. There are degrees of Life in form, but Life in Itself is impersonal, expressing Itself through the form created by Life Itself.

46. The mighty Intelligence of the Infinite Father has created all forms for His own self-expression. The Life is the same ; It flows only from the One Source, yet It flows through all the forms It created. It is manifesting in every

form from the smallest to the greatest ; Life is manifesting Itself in every form It creates.

47. Nothing comes into being except by the Spirit which is Life. The degree of Life is understood through the recognition and realisation of It ; therefore, as I realise Life and know It to be God, He manifests through me according to my realisation of Him who created us in His own likeness.

48. The recognition and realisation of His Life in your own consciousness becomes the means through which Life manifests. Your consciousness is the point through which God expresses Himself and is the point through which you express God the Christ in you.

49. If you are consciously aware of this, then you have gained the hidden secret of Life Itself.

50. It is hidden from the multitude, even to-day, except to those who know they are not born of the flesh nor by the will of man but through the Christ of God.

51. Therefore I am that Life ; I have all power given unto me in heaven and on earth. " Seek ye first the Kingdom of God and His righteousness and all things shall be added unto you."

52. Consciousness determines the degree of Life being expressed. I am conscious that I am the Life of God, " I am the Christ of God," " I am the true Son of the Father who worketh in me."

53. The Christ Consciousness reveals the Father having dominion over all things in heaven and on earth. This is truly Christ Consciousness.

54. It was for this purpose that I lived upon earth and am still with you, even unto the end of the world, that is, until all shall recognise and realise the Christ Consciousness so that we may all be one.

55. That we may all be one through the realisation and recognition of the Truth I wait patiently. You do not

quarrel over that which is true ; you quarrel only over that which is false ; you do not quarrel over the fact that you are alive, living ; you quarrel only over your beliefs, your ideas. That which is mortal is seeking a way out of the carnal world into that which is greater, so the mortal argues with himself, but the Christ never argues ; he knows. Therefore it is easy to discern that which is false from that which is true.

56. The sacred word is " I am." " I am that I am," the prophets knew through the ages, the eternal secret. Yet only a few could understand. But all will come to understand, for it is the decree of the Father that the son shall reveal Him, so that all shall know Him. And He who does the will of my Father is my mother, my sister, my brother.

57. As one realises more and more the power of the Christ, one sees clearly that His Power must be Love and Wisdom, because the Christ is the Son of God. When I said that I did not come to destroy the Law but to fulfil the Law, this was true, for I did bring the message of the great Power in heaven to earth—the Power of the Christ within to the outer, and this power is Love and Wisdom. It is the builder of all good things like harmony and peace. It remains forever, while discord remains only in ignorance, which is death and not Life.

58. I want you to give some part of the day to this silent growth, thus bringing poise and balance into your whole being. This is so essential in your daily lives surrounded by the din of social problems and the rumours of war.

59. First, you will be conscious of the quiet feeling of the Presence, a stillness that is ever active. How beautiful is the silence in that ever active presence of God, the expression of His Mighty Power and harmony in your lives. This will develop in you a good sound judgment, and clear insight, and afterwards the result will be established in your body and circumstances.

60. Silence in the heart of flesh will become united with the heart of Spirit and thus bring about perfect circulation of the blood.

61. Thank the Father for His counsel, for teaching you every day.

62. Keep the Father at all times before you. With Him in your heart you cannot fail. Some think that by themselves they can accomplish, yet only with God can you accomplish anything.

63. Is your mind always in a state of wanting ? And never in a state of giving ? Yet giving is receiving. To be one with the Father you have to open yourself to Him and to allow the precious Power of Love and Wisdom to flow through you. He alone is the supplier of all things ; without Him there is not anything made that is made.

64. And when your heart and soul rejoice, your body rests secure, and every fibre tingles with the Presence, for the Presence of God is omnipresent.

65. The full joy of His Presence and the bliss of being with Him forever will develop the Christ Consciousness more than anything else. Do not look without, but look within and know yourself to BE. I am. I am real, I am eternal, I am the Spirit of God, I am the Life ; in this realisation the soul rejoices. This only comes when the noise from outside quietens down when you discern all that is not of God.

66. The Spirit of the Living God, the Christ, breathes through the outer body of flesh from within. Divine energies always express themselves from within and never from without.

67. The brain is fed by the Spirit, the finer rules over the grosser, the invisible flows through the visible. The visible is but the expression of the invisible. No one has seen the Father, but you have seen His son and he who has seen me has seen the Father.

68. I am making this plain to you so as to make you realise the importance of selecting periods for quiet contemplation so as to bring into the outer the power within.

69. Come out from your busy-day life and enter into the Kingdom and become aware of Who is working in and through you. To become conscious of His power renews your body, renews your mind, and brings peace and Love into your heart. You will find that things around you will move much easier, conditions that exist in your mind, body and circumstances will begin to harmonise with your realisation of the Christ, the power that has dominion over all things.

70. Later when you have become conscious of the Father in you as your Reality, you will be in command at all times, heeding neither discord nor environment, for the Christ within shall be enthroned in the heart and mind.

71. Periods of quiet contemplation and realisation bring into your consciousness the completeness of the Christ, then you shall not heed conditions outside yourself. Inharmony will not affect you; you will be quiet and at peace with that which is in Itself Love, Peace, Wisdom and Truth Eternal.

72. Do not seek Love! Give it! This is the true nourishment of the Spirit, for wherever love is, hate and envy and jealousy disappear.

73. Remember, Love casteth out fear, neither rebel against injustice. When you return Love you are at peace, then only does the Father work to overcome all things. When you resent injustice, when your mind is in a state of turmoil, full of envy, jealousy, anxiety, resentment, there is no Love; Love is the only power in the world that dissolves all these things.

74. It is only possible for the Father to express Himself in you when you are at peace.

75. The only power that exists is the Power of Love,

which brings Peace and Harmony ; all other things pass away and dissolve into nothingness before the power of the Christ. I am the Lord, I have overcome all things, and so shall you. Nothing can harm you, for you are God's in the flesh.

76. If you will listen to this, my brothers and sisters, you can take from your Father what is your right. '' What is Mine is Thine, what is Thine is Mine.''

77. God brought you into this world, and every moment He is speaking in your hearts. Every beat of your heart is the Life of God in you. With Him consciously in your heart you will be at peace with all men. To Love thy neighbour as thyself is true religion.

78. For everyone that is illuminated turns into light. Therefore, wake up, O sleeper, and rise from the dead, and Christ will shine in your countenance.

79. Be strictly careful to act as sensible sons and daughters of God, and make the most of your time in the '' now,'' for now is eternity.

80. You think in the Eternal when you think with Christ. Think in the Eternal now, for you can only create in the now. Oh, could I make it so plain to you that you could see it clearly—NOW is eternity.

81. This brings me to the last point in this talk : '' Prayer.'' Prayer to me was and is the breathing of the breath of Life. It is the most powerful thing in all planes and in all worlds.

82. The power of prayer lies in the fact that the prayer and the answer are one. Pray with the realisation that you are one with the Father, and the Father's will is done in you. Enter into your Divine Centre within where God dwells, and there I will proclaim for you.

83. I am pleased to see that you have not used this powerful weapon ignorantly. Our beloved brother was taught to pray when he was young. I could tell you many

things that have happened in his life, because he was guided when he was a young child. He was born a medium and saw me face to face when quite a youth. That is one of his many experiences. He was brought to the Himalayas for the purpose of learning how to become a medium through which the Masters could speak, and therefore I myself could overshadow him.

84. The time came for him to go out into the world ; he has been blest with good health, his spirit is young, and we hope to keep him in the body for a long time to come, for his work here on earth is not yet finished.

85. Most prayers are often sent with the false idea of separation, and in your churches and chapels this is most evident, the belief being that God is afar off. Yet He is nearer than hands and feet.

86. But even this prayer is never lost, although its full value is not gained, because a prayer of this kind mingles with the vibration of separation and the person you desire to help is not helped to any great extent.

87. Enter into your closet where the Almighty dwells and there see the will of God accomplished. Never see or hear anything else. Without strain or doubt see the victory of the Christ, the only begotten Son of God, accomplished in those you wish to help, and it will be established.

88. There are accounts of healings in my records which many of you have read ; these healings are brought about by the same means, the recognition and the realisation of the power having dominion over all things, the flesh having no say in the matter.

89. When you speak from the Christ in the strength of your calm assurance, the false condition completely disappears. God is omnipresent and you bring the troubled Spirit in touch with God instantly.

90. You cannot estimate the value of true prayer.

Words fail to express Spiritual realities. Do not cast your burden upon an outside God, waiting for results, wondering ; for God is within you, the prayer and the answer are as one.

91. God is the only Life Living in and through all, God is the Reality ; the mortal sense knows nothing of Him. The inner must become the outer, and the outer must become the inner. In this way pray : " Father, Thou knowest me ; I know that Thou art the only Living Being, the only Creator, and I am one with Thee. As I ask of Thee, I know it is already accomplished ; my word does not return unto me void but accomplishes that which it is sent forth to do."

92. To know God in your own heart, and in the utmost space, is to be at " one " with all nations, north, south, east and west.

93. Live in the thought of Love towards all, and your life will become one continuous prayer, a constant going forth from God the Father of all, to all.

94. My blessing is with you always and forever.

MY PEACE AND LOVE I LEAVE WITH YOU

SILENCE

Benediction

The will of our Father in heaven is now being done on earth. Peace be with you.

———————

(THE SCRIBE'S REMARKS :

A great power was felt by all and the hall became alight with a light that was not of earth. The Master's face was seen clearly in the midst of a brilliant light overshadowing the Brother's face. Then the Master took his departure, and the brother was seen standing in the place where the Master overshadowed him.)

TALK 4

I am the True Vine and You are the Branches

My peace I bring to you, my peace remain with you.

1. I am the true vine and my Father is the worker. It is the Father, Who ever remaineth within me, Who is working through me, for the Father and I are one ; we are never separated. We continually work together and what I see the Father do, I do likewise.

2. The branch that bears fruit He prunes, so that it may bring forth more fruit.

3. You all know that a branch that bears fruit will bring more fruit when that branch is pruned.

4. The branch is you, and you are pruned because of the word I have given to you : the word that was in the beginning, and that very word is God.

5. You will realise now that there is no other living Being but the Father, the Father of all, and the Spirit of the Father dwelleth in every living soul ; and I am that Spirit.

6. God is Spirit, not " a " Spirit, but Spirit. Spirit in Itself is complete, It has the power to manifest, to create the forms for its own expression. And as you become conscious of Reality you become one with Reality in expression.

7. This realisation and recognition does not come all at once. You will notice how it grows in you. By diligent recognition and continual realisation, there is an awakening within the soul as the soul begins to recognise that it is the Spirit of God that dwells within and is the only living Creative Power in heaven and on earth.

8. You have already been pruned because of the word I have given to you ; therefore you will bear more fruit in my name.

9. I remain with you and you remain with me ; just as a branch cannot bear fruit by itself unless it remains in the vine, so you cannot bear fruit unless you remain with me.

10. The Christ alone has the power to speak in Reality. Then speak in the name of Christ and your word will not return unto you void.

11. The Christ never speaks from mortal sense or from the reaction to things external to Itself, but Christ always speaks from God, and this you must also learn, so that you can quiet the outside. The still quiet voice is made manifest in the Temple not made with hands but by God Himself.

12. The Father worketh in the vine so that the branches bear good fruit, and these who remain with me and I with them will bear abundant fruit.

13. If therefore you remain with me and my word remains with you, whatever you ask shall be done unto you.

14. You have not yet grasped the great significance of what I have said. The Christ never begs, nor does the Christ demand, nor does the Christ command ; the Christ manifests, because the Christ knows that it is the Father who doeth the work.

15. The son hath Life in himself only because the Father has Life in Himself, the Life that is now eternally in Himself He gives It also eternally to the son. The same Life in the Father is the same Life in the son.

16. In this way the Father will be glorified, that you bear abundant fruit and be my disciples.

17. And as the Father has loved me, so have I loved you, that you may remain in this love.

18. To remain in my love is the secret of all happiness ; without it, your life is barren.

19. When the Christ dwells in the heart, then there is Love, Wisdom and Power, and the things that trouble you will pass away, for the Christ overcomes all.

20. In this your joy will be full. For you did not choose me, I chose you.

21. It is I who live within you who is guiding you and helping you to choose the way, I urge you to recognise the truth of the only " one " Living God.

22. Therefore Love one another as I love you.

23. There are those of the world who, not knowing me, will hate and say things against you. Know well that I was hated and despised before you. The ignorance of the world is still in the world and it is the Christ that will overcome this ignorance through Love, and the Christ lives in you. Yet this ignorance will hate you, will despise you because you say that the Christ lives in you, but verily I say, fear not, for ignorance has no power, it cannot destroy the soul nor the Spirit.

24. It cannot destroy that which it cannot see and does not know. It did not destroy me when it crucified me, it could not destroy the soul nor the Spirit, nor could it destroy the Light it did not know ; therefore I am still alive, the living Christ of God, the only begotten Son of the Father.

25. You know now that you are not of the world, that you are born of the Spirit, and the Christ dwells in you, but the world is yet ignorant of the truth.

26. But the Spirit of Truth which proceeds from the Father will testify concerning me, and you will also testify because you have been with me from the beginning.

27. If you will seek deep enough within yourselves you will find this truth, this truth shall testify regarding me, and this Truth shall set you free.

28. My word in you will glorify Him who sent me, and you will be glorified by me in His presence.

29. If my disciples were to keep me they would lose the Christ of God, for I came to reveal the Father, so that I may come and abide with you all forever.

30. You who have passed beyond the plane of mortal sense and entered into that greater consciousness of Life understand more of God.

31. You realise the great truth that there is no death, that you are still living, yet once dwelt in a body on earth.

32. You are Life, you are the living expression of the Almighty. This Life in you is the same Life in me. This is the Christ and I speak from the Christ that is Life.

33. If your faith is great, whatever you wish will be established at that very hour.

34. These words are full of meaning and become greater when you know that I can come to all in the omnipotence of the Christ.

35. I have shown you already that Spirit is our first and only real foundation.

36. It has many channels and modes of expression, but it is the one and only Life, the only Creative Power.

37. Through your consciousness this power is expressed.

38. Let me explain to you how you hear me now.

39. Through recognition and realisation of the Truth that Life is one, that the Father alone is the Consciousness in you and me, and is expressing Himself through His creation in this way.

40. The only way that the Creator can express Himself in all His creations is through His Consciousness, becoming aware of His creation, and His awareness in His creation becomes the Consciousness in you and me.

41. I enter the Life Consciousness being expressed through our brother ; my Consciousness overshadows his, just as a greater light overshadows the lesser, yet the same Source-Light shines in us both.

42. Here is a most wonderful manifestation, some people will say phenomena, but really there is no phenomenon but the expression of that one Life becoming aware of Itself through the Consciousness of another.

43. The brother is able to take his departure from his body at any time. He does not really take his departure as one would say, but recedes from the outer Consciousness into the inner Consciousness and by receding into the inner Consciousness is able to come in contact with you at any time.

44. He is able to treat you, to help you, he is able to call upon me at any time to bring more aid and help when it is necessary.

45. Therefore, through the Sanctuary, silent healing work is being done all over the world. And as the consciousness in man becomes more aware of this tremendous power that is within, it begins to express this power.

46. Infinite eternal and perfect Love is in the world, because God is Love and Love is God, and the consciousness must become aware of this to express true Love, the secret of Divine Bliss.

47. The Consciousness of the brother is lifted from the personal to the Universal, yet this does not mean loss of identity but a greater amount of individuality in unity with the All.

48. The Christ is the individuality of the Father being expressed ; there is no separation between the Christ and the Father, for they are one. The Father being expressed in individuality is the Christ in you now.

49. But as the Christ recedes into the consciousness of the Life that dwells everywhere, thus I can come to all of you in the omnipotence of the Father. And whoever asks anything in my name it shall be done, for the Father and I are one.

50. In this way your consciousness is also lifted up.

The consciousness of man must be lifted up to recognise the Consciousness of God. And it is through these talks that your consciousness is being raised from the consciousness of the self to recognise the Consciousness of God, the indwelling Christ.

51. The Lord dwells in His holy Temple : the Temple not made with hands but by the word that flows from the mouth of God and " I am that Word, nothing has come into being except through me."

52. You must realise the Consciousness of God within yourselves, because through that alone have you come into being.

53. Man on the plane of mortal sense has tried to explain with his finite mind the Infinite wisdom and love of God.

54. Would you, in your new knowledge, dare to limit the Holy One to that of a person ? Man who does not know himself dares to explain the whole of God !

55. Your faith must not rest in the wisdom of man but in the power and love and wisdom of God.

56. The Love, Wisdom and Power of God existed before the world was. But none of the rulers of the world knew it. Had they known it they would not have crucified me.

57. Yet through my crucifixion all will come to know the truth that I was before the world was formed. The Spirit of God was before the world was formed, and the Spirit has been made flesh and dwells on earth, yet the same Spirit dwells in Heaven.

58. For it was by me and through me that the world became form. This was the wisdom of God the Father being expressed through the Son, the Son of the very living God, " and I am He that liveth in you."

59. It is written that the eye has not seen, and the ear has not heard, and the heart of man has not conceived, the things that God has prepared for them who love Him.

60. Yet God has revealed them to me by His Spirit, for the Spirit searches and reveals everything, even the depths of God.

61. It is the Christ that is within, that knoweth the mind of man, and no one knoweth the Mind of God except the Spirit of God.

62. Know that the Christ discerns everything, yet no one can describe Him. It is the Christ that discerns the false. It is the Christ that knows the true. The Christ, being all-powerful, dissolves the ignorance in the world.

63. Around you at this moment there are probably a quarter of a million souls listening to my talks, many of them are mingling with yourselves.

64. You hear my voice here upon the physical, yet in the inner planes my voice is also heard ; in the higher spiritual planes my voice is also heard, also by many who are just awakening to the Truth of the Christ within themselves.

65. I am the Christ of God, the very Spirit of God that was before the world began, and through me all things that came to be, were created.

66. If you seek deep enough within yourselves you will learn of Him Who is greatest in His meekness, and highest in His lowliness.

67. Your personality becomes clear as you learn to realise your relationship to the whole.

68. Your mind clears as you become filled with holy reverence, the heart centre is filled with light. The weakest and the lowliest and the meekest person has the whole Universe to draw upon.

69. No matter who you are, or what you are, remember that the Christ dwells in you. The Christ is often hidden by the ignorance of mortal sense that can only hear from without, but, if you will awaken to the Christ within, the

still quiet voice that is all-power will manifest itself through you. This awakening is the realisation of your oneness with all, with God who is all.

70. For this is my son that was dead and has come to Life, was lost and now found.

71. For heaven is more joyful over one that was once lost and now found than ninety-nine that did not stray.

72. Many are angry because the Father loveth the lost sheep, yet I say unto you, that one hath more need of the Father's love. Believe in me and know that the Love of God is expressed through me and that I love everyone, even those who despised me.

73. My awareness of God is never clouded by injustice done ; my awareness and understanding of the Father's love enables me to enter into that true state where I could say, " Father, forgive them, for they know not what they do."

74. There are those who may not have strayed from the fold, yet are unable to partake of the gifts the Father provides for all who love Him, because they do not know that they are always with Him.

75. They call and cry out with a loud voice to God, thinking that He may hear them from afar off. But I tell you that " I am He who lives and dwells in you, I am the son of God, I am the Light of the World. I am the true individuality of the Father, and whatever I ask of the Father the Father will provide." If you can ask then in my name, recognising me in yourselves, whatever you ask will be done unto you.

76. The Father is always saying in your heart, if you will but hear Him, " My son, you are always with Me and everything that is Mine is thine."

77. You exist because God Is, and all He has is yours.

78. Many of you seem to lack vitality ; this is because you live an unequal existence in the three planes of

manifestation, Spiritual, Mental and Physical, or Spirit, Soul and Body.

79. This unequal state of existence is brought about by your belief in the fact that Life is derived from some external source.

80. The majority of you pay too much attention to the body and too little attention to the Source of Life.

81. You should recognise first that Spirit is the only Source of Life and vitality. Draw from that Source first, then the soul and body will be nourished and fed.

82. It is God Who inspires you with the will to do the good things you desire to do, and the power to do so is according to your understanding, for God is always inspiring you to do His will.

83. To love God you must also love your neighbour, because God is your neighbour. If you love Me then you must love those around you, because they are also Me. You have been given free will to act according to the Law known to yourselves, but, when the Christ is on the throne, then the Christ manifests perfectly. Let this Christ in you be enthroned in the Holy Temple, the Temple of the Living God not made with hands.

84. The secret of accomplishment is to do all things without disputing and doubting. This brings into operation the Creative Power to accomplish.

85. Only on earth can you do this great work ; you do not know yet how important it is to work now. Spirit cannot be separated from Spirit ; It is indivisible.

86. I want these talks to help you to enter into your own now.

87. If you realise that the Spirit of the Christ is omnipotent, omnipresent, and omniscient, then why do you wait ? It is wrong for you to hope and expect the grace of God only in some future time.

88. The Spirit in you is the Christ of God, and Spirit

cannot be less than the greatest ; then let the Christ in you take possession of your soul and body and all you hoped for will come to pass.

89. Remember the word was in the beginning and that very word was God, and God was that word ; then be true to that word.

90. Remember the word was in the beginning and that word was made flesh and dwelt amongst us.

91. Your thoughts are the outbreathing of this word, the first Cause of All. " I am the word, and my word does not return to me void but accomplishes that which it is sent forth to do."

92. The Spirit is always revealing me, the Christ of God, and the Spirit will lead you into all Truth. It is the Truth that sets you free. Nothing else can set you free except the Truth of the Almighty God. And when the truth of the Christ dwells in you, the word that was in the beginning, the word that is made flesh, then there is no longer any fear or doubt.

93. There are many who allow antagonisms to enter into the heart and mind, and prevent the Christ from manifesting.

94. Let this Christ then dwell in your heart and be the light that shines in your soul—then it will not be lip-service. You work in God ; you are the branches ; and you are being pruned so that you will bring forth more fruit.

95. " I AM " the word that prunes you.

96. Do you recognise the meaning of my words ?   " I speak not as a mortal but as the Christ of God. I lift you from your mortal sense into a Spiritual state of consciousness so that you will understand me."

97. Your healing took place when God spoke in His Holy Temple and all the senses were silenced by the Presence of His quiet still voice.

98. All outside personalities cease to touch you when you enter into this blessed state of the Christ within. " I am He who was in the beginning and is now and for evermore shall be."

(SILENCE while heavenly music and singing are heard.)

99. Many of your loved ones who dwelt with you on earth have entered into the larger sphere of Life's consciousness and are with you here now. They have gathered around you and can get closer to you as you listen to me.

100. Little you know how close they are. They watch and pray with you.

101. Listen to my word and you will understand the inner Voice so that your Life will be full, your bodies perfectly whole. You will be safe from harm or accident, for the veil that divides us is very thin.

102. You can pierce it with your thoughts, and thus we can come to you ; this—and more—will be revealed unto you, " for I am with you always, even unto the end of the world."

103. And as you listen to me I will teach you. Do you think that I am afar off ? Do you think there is a division in space that separates us ?

104. There is no separation in Christ ; there is no separation in that " One " Life that lives through all. God has not divided Himself, He has individualised Himself, but this is not division. It is individuality in unity.

105. God created nothing separate from Himself, but through me He expresses Himself, and I am His son. He who listens to me free from limitation shall know my voice, for I speak for the Father Himself who ever remains within me.

106. Let us now enter into the Sanctuary of the Silent Healing Power. I want you to keep your eyes open, and

look towards me and you will realise the Christ that lives in each and every one of you.

107. Seek first the Love and Wisdom of God, and all things shall be added unto you.

(THE SCRIBE'S REMARKS:

In the Silence a brilliant light lights up the whole of the auditorium. The face of the Master becomes so bright that we cannot gaze upon the Master's face. Then he takes his departure with the words

MY PEACE AND MY LOVE REMAIN WITH YOU.)

TALK 5

Because I Live You shall Live also

My peace, my love I bring to you ; because I live, you shall
live in me and I in you—this is Eternal Life.

1. There is nothing in life that you need fear. Leave
all to the Father and be patient. Many of you fear this
and that, because you are not aware of the Christ within.

2. If you are filled with fear, this causes you to
waver. Therefore you often do the wrong thing which may
affect your personal life ; not that it matters very much,
because Life is the only Reality, and in the end all things
move in the right direction.

3. But if you fear not and be patient, the Father will
take His place in you, and I shall be with Him, and you
shall be free now.

4. Know that you live in God and God lives in you ;
there is no outside, and there is nowhere where God is
not. There you are safe at all times in every place, when
this Truth is truly known.

5. Oh, could I make you understand that it is God who
is living in you and through you, the Father Himself,
His Consciousness, His Life, His Intelligence, and in His
Wisdom He is continually expressing Himself in and
through you. If you will but realise this wonderful Truth
you will know that there is no place where He is not ;
He is omnipresent, He is everywhere ; and wherever you
are, so is He.

6. The secret of power is within your own consciousness
because the Consciousness of God, the Intelligence of God,
is expressing Itself through you, making you the sons and
daughters of God.

7. Let the mortal sense be silent, then the Christ in you will take possession of your mortal body. When the mortal sense is active, the Christ in you is silent.

8. There is nothing to fear, so be patient and let the Father speak for you. For it is the Father in me that speaketh. I myself am nothing, but the Father that dwelleth in me is all. The Father knoweth me, I know the Father, and because I knoweth the Father the Father speaketh in me and through me. Thus I bring His peace and His love, His healing and His wisdom.

9. The Father is always revealing Himself in me to you, for " I am the Life." I AM THE LIFE; the word that was in the beginning.

10. Many have refused to accept me as the Saviour of the Race. Yet I am the Life, the Life of the Father is in the Son, the only Reality.

11. I revealed the Father in His Love, in His Power, in His Wisdom, His Eternal Life, and I come to give freely of the Father Who sent me. This is the saving of the race.

12. I do not speak from the flesh ; I speak from the Consciousness of God ; in God I dwell eternally, and it is the Father in me that speaketh to you now.

13. And if ye will accept my " word " you will be free. Just as the " Living " Father sent me, I am living because of the Father, so whosoever eats of me will also live because of me.

14. To eat of me means to take me into yourselves, to be within yourselves, and I shall be in you, and you shall be in me and we all in the Father.

15. I am always knocking at the door of your heart and you will always find me there waiting patiently. And when you open the door of your heart and mind, then I shall enter in and abide with you forever, and you shall be with me.

16. This is the Bread which comes down from heaven and he who eats of this Bread shall live for ever.

17. I am living, and the promise I have made is the Father's word ; therefore you shall live forever ; for in me there is no death, for I am the Life.

18. Perhaps some of you have not yet grasped what I have said and you stumble at my word.

19. The Spirit of God in man is " I am." You will observe if you read the Old Testament where Moses perceived the burning bush, and out of the burning bush the voice spoke " I am." This was the secret word of Power given to the prophets, and told to the multitude. It was on their lips but they did not know it, but he who could understand entered into the wisdom of the prophets.

20. The Spirit of God in man is " I am," I am Spirit, and the Spirit ascends whence it came. It is the Spirit that gives life—the body has no life in itself ; and the words I have spoken to you are Spirit and Life.

21. I am the Bread of Life that comes down from heaven and has entered the world of flesh to give it Life.

22. Heaven is not a place ; it is an inner consciousness, an inner knowing of Reality ; and this inner knowing of Reality is known as the heaven that is above, just as the earth is below.

23. The earth is but the manifestation of the inner realms, and the Life that animates it comes from within and expresses Itself outwardly.

24. The inner consciousness is heaven expressing itself through the body upon earth. I know, and you know now, that you are one with me. I am in heaven and when you understand me you shall be in heaven also, even now.

25. I am in you and you are in me, therefore, if ye eat of my body and drink of my blood ye shall be with me, for I shall be in you and you in me, thus you will remember me.

26. My words have been misunderstood because I

speak from the Life within. When I speak from Life I do not mean the flesh, for the flesh has no say in the matter.

27. My Spiritual body is substance and is perfect ; it is the Spiritual body alone that gives the flesh sustenance. If you drink of me—my Life—you will take me into yourselves. If you eat of my body—my wisdom—then my wisdom shall be in you and I will be with you always, thus you will remember me.

28. My teaching is not mine but the Father's who liveth in me. He speaketh for me.

29. Now you know me, and you know whence I come, yet I have not come of my own accord but from Him who sent me and He is true. It is He the Father whom I reveal to you. I do the will of my Father and my Father's will is done in me.

30. I know Him because I am from Him and He sent me, yet we are " one." " The Father and I are one."

31. The time will come when I will reveal the Father to all peoples of the earth, and there shall be no more wailing or gnashing of teeth.

32. There will be rejoicing among the nations, for they will know the truth about " our " Father which is in Heaven. OUR Father of Love and Wisdom.

33. Everyone shall forgive one another, for only through forgiveness and love can you enter into the joy of the Father's House.

34. Do you understand what that really means ? Have you ever felt the joy of being in the Father's House ? Only when you can express that Divine Love which frees you from all that is untrue, is the Blessedness of the Father the Christ revealed in you. Can you realise now the joy of being in the Father's House now and forever more ?

35. And all shall partake of their daily portion of the bread of Life that comes down from heaven. This bread is the true bread, the Life, " and I am that Life."

36. I have said before to you, "Forgive ye one another." I have also said to you, "Love ye one another."

37. My words are true, for the Father loves each and every one with an everlasting Love and with the same Love ye must love one another.

38. His love is mighty, powerful, overwhelming. If His love is in you, there is the joy of the Father. May His love and peace reign in you always.

39. For your entire will, thought, and brain are led by this holy invisible Spirit into the knowledge of all truth.

40. His will that is done in heaven shall also be done on earth through you. In your own hearts the Will of My Father is done.

41. The inner realms of my consciousness shall proceed to the outer, and the mortal sense shall be silenced, and the Christ shall take His place in the world to redeem it.

42. Your present state is one of training and unfoldment. You learn lessons of childhood before you become adult.

43. You are passing through the stages now, and you will arrive at the true awareness in your heart and mind, of the Christ within that is all-power, filled with the Father's love.

44. Listen to me and read my words and they will have a new meaning each time you read them. I will repeat the Truth in many different ways till you begin to understand.

45. Then you shall be filled with my knowing. My words are life, and they will strengthen your heart and mind in your daily living.

46. Read them quietly and calmly in your quiet hour, and they they will remain with you.

47. When I speak you know I speak the truth, for you feel the truth of my words in yourselves. Every word I speak is true, yet I know you do not hold on to my word always.

48. Now that you have seen me and heard me, and I have given to you what my Father gave to me, thus you shall remember my words. My words shall remain with you and when you remember my words you will remember me.

49. All come to me, for to die to the body is to live with the Lord.

50. Already you are entering into the wider knowledge. Blessed are you who heareth these words for many have passed from the body ignorant of much with which you are familiar.

51. Many listening to me, yet invisible to you, have passed from the earthly body not understanding the truth that Life is Eternal. Life is not interrupted by the event called death ; there is no break in life, in birth or in death.

52. Remember there is no birth and no death in life. These invisible ones who are around you, and above you, know now that there is no division in Life, neither is there separation between those who have left the body and those who are still in the body. This is the Christ, I am the Life, the Father who ever remaineth with Me, He is the Father that ever remaineth within you also, and in the Father there is no death, no separation.

53. You are indestructible spiritual beings and this truth alters your whole mental attitude towards sickness and death.

54. Ask yourselves this question and satisfy yourselves in regard to it : " Whom am I ? " It is a pertinent question ; therefore search deep into your heart and mind and you shall find the answer.

55. " You are because God is." There can be no separation between you and me and the Father, for we are all one. There is no separation because there is no outside of God. There is no division in God.

56. You have become individuals because the Father

has individualised Himself in you ; thus you reveal the Life of the Father.

57. Where you are at the moment is because God is where you are, and no one else can fill your place in the perfect Cosmic scheme.

58. I come to do the work the Father hath sent me to do.

59. Do not rebel against conditions but learn your lessons from them.

60. Your mortal sense blinds you to this truth because you look without instead of looking within.

61. When you look within, you find the Christ ; and by your oneness with the Father you spiritualise all things, and confusion disappears. All is made real by the presence of the Christ in you.

62. I use my power wisely because the Father guideth me ; therefore my love goes out to everyone because I know the Father is love and loves all His creation. Only the mortal sense fails to understand my Love and peace towards all.

63. Remember there is no separation between you and me or between you and those who have left the mortal body.

64. Fear is the only barrier, and this fear exists only in your mind ; it is not a reality, it is of your own creation by your reaction to the outer while not knowing the inner.

65. For the Father reigneth forever and He through me conquers all enemies ; and the last enemy is fear of so-called death. With this fear gone, all is made anew through the Christ within.

66. The son is also subject unto the Father, for the Father is all in all. I of myself am nothing ; it is the Spirit of the Father within me that doeth the work.

67. Hold this attitude of mind and heart so that you can receive me. Through this attitude of mind and heart

the Father who ever remaineth in me also remaineth in you. He will do for you what He doeth for me.

68. For all the good exists forever, and this good surrounds you and can never change or be lost.

69. This good is only harmed because your eyes perceive good and evil ; the only Real is that which is, and not that which is not. God is all there is ; there is no other living Being but He. He created heaven and earth and all that lives therein and thereon.

70. My word is good, it produces good fruit ; this word is everlasting because it comes from Him who sent me.

71. Whosoever hears this word and does not hold on to It, It is snatched away. This is like the seed that was sown by the roadside and failed to take root.

72. There are others who hear my word of the Kingdom within. They immediately accept it and are joyful, but it does not take root except for a little while, and is then forgotten ; and when trouble comes, it dies because the roots are not deep enough. This is like the seed that falls in stony ground.

73. When you do not hold on to the word it is snatched away from you because it has not taken root in your soul. The word must penetrate deep into your soul and there take root and be held fast by faith.

74. The word is " I am the Life." I have dominion over all things. All power has been given unto me in heaven and on earth.

75. Riches may also choke the word because of worldly desires and deception ; these are the thistles that choke the growth. Think over these words of mine earnestly.

76. You have heard the word and now you understand it ; so it grows in good soil and bears fruit, for you are the good soil that produces, some of you one hundred, some sixty, some thirty.

77. As I told you, the last time we gathered together, you did not choose me but I chose you.

78. Now when I sow my seed in you and you accept my word and this word dwells in you, I am in you and you are in Me.

79. My word is the leaven in you, and as you allow it to work in you, you become leaven.

80. My word will spring up in you. It is the spring of everlasting Life, it will flood your soul and body and we will breathe and think as one. Thus you shall eat of my body and drink of my blood ; thus you shall remember me.

81. I bring out secrets hidden in you before the foundation of the world.

82. Your work you have undertaken from the beginning and every step you take is the right one. You perhaps do not see the end, and thus you doubt ; but even your doubt cannot stop the creative scheme to alter and change.

83. Never be discouraged by appearances, always see the good to which all shall attain. Know that the eternal scheme must be fulfilled, because it is the will of God. The glory and purpose behind it, is love, peace, harmony, goodwill towards all men.

84. You are on earth at present to help in this work. That is why I have come to you. I am with you, helping you always. Perhaps you have not realised this fully, yet these words of mine are true, and whatever you ask of me believing, so it shall be done unto you.

85. Know that God is Incarnate Love, and Love never fails, but makes all things anew.

86. If you believe that I am he who spoke through the mouth of Jesus and accept me now, you will do much in my name, for I am always with you, and with me is the Father who sent me.

87. It is the Father who is living ; I live because He

lives in me. You live also because of Him ; I live in the Father, and the Father lives in me, and I live in you and we all live in the Father.

88. Call no man your Father on earth for one is your Father who is in Heaven.

89. He who does not believe in the Son of God and rejects him does not know himself.

90. The more you know of me and my Father, the greater becomes your reverence for the exquisite wisdom and order in every created thing.

91. The very stones and rocks are marvels of His creation ; every drop of dew obeys His law and fulfils His eternal purpose.

92. As you open up to the word that was in the beginning, you will discern the higher laws and become in harmony with them.

93. You may make mistakes but these become experiences to aid you. Fear not, nor regret the past ; know that the mighty Eternal Love is seeking expression everywhere now.

94. I am the Light in man and those who follow me shall not walk in darkness : I am the Light of the World.

95. I reveal the Father in all His glory to you. It is for this purpose I have come.

96. The Pharisees said, " You testify concerning yourself, your testimony is not true."

97. They did not know the Spirit of God, neither did they know whence I came or whither I go. I knew whence I came and whither I go.

98. I knew I came from God ; I knew He sent me into the world. I knew the world would deny me, yet by denying me the world is forced to accept me. But let me tell you this : to deny me is to deny the Father who sent me. I am the Life of the Father, the Consciousness of God expressing Himself in man.

99. Men judge according to the flesh, but I judge no one : and if I should judge, my judgment is true, because I am not alone, for my Father is always with me.

100. I testify not concerning myself, my Father who sent me testifies concerning me, and if you accept me you accept my Father also. Realise that there is no separation, then you shall know me.

101. The Christ always meets the need of people at their exact degree of unfoldment.

102. Thus I never fail to help if you will but believe, for the Love of the Father meets every need, for He knows what you are in need of before you ask. This is the eternal promise that exists to all those who believe in me.

103. When you love with all your heart, soul, mind and strength I shall reign in you, and nothing will be impossible to you.

104. The Love of the Father in me is expressed in you. In that Love there is Intelligence, Power and Wisdom to accomplish all things.

105. Do not fail to understand that the Spiritual body is perfect substance and every part of your material body will act in obedience to the Christ, the only *Reality*.

106. Should you suffer, suffer in peace, and I shall reign in your life, for God is working in your midst and cannot fail; then your suffering shall not be in vain. You shall feel the power of the Christ, and your sufferings shall be no more. With me, your yoke is light.

107. The Father liveth with me in your life, even while in the flesh ; therefore live by the word that is in you. I who love you have given myself for you, and where I am there you shall be also.

MY PEACE AND MY LOVE I LEAVE WITH YOU.

(SILENCE)

(THE SCRIBE'S REMARKS:

Before the Master took his departure the same bright light is seen, and there on each side of the Master appear two of his disciples, one on each side, and as they left the music and the singing died away. The students remained sitting for some time, spellbound by the wonderful experience.)

TALK 6

The Spirit of the Father who Raised me from the "Dead" Dwells within You

1. The Spirit of the Father who raised me from the "dead" dwells within you.

2. Perhaps you do not realise the importance of these words. But it is the same Spirit and there is no division in Spirit, the one Spirit manifesting in the many and that many in the One.

3. It was this mighty power that I saw completely in my own life and, by the recognition of it, so was I able to use the power of the Spirit of God the Father Who dwelt within me ; this Spirit of the Father who raised me from the dead is within you also.

4. When your mortal sense would indicate disorder, pain and death, remember the Spirit of the Father which remaineth within you.

5. Call It into manifestation by the word of power "I am." Have you fully realised the meaning of the word "I am"?

6. You cannot speak the word "I am" in Reality unless you know the meaning of It, and when you know the meaning of the word "I am" you have learnt the word of power. "I am the Life." I am living because His Life liveth in me. Life is God and God is Life.

7. Therefore my Spirit will quicken your mortal flesh and the Satan of the senses shall be under your feet.

8. It has always been the Satan of the senses that has blinded you to the real truth of the immanent power of the Spirit that dwells within.

9. The senses reveal to you things from without, but the Spirit of God reveals the Truth from within, and not having this Truth you are powerless.

10. The mortal sense only sees things from without, and that which it sees it does not know what it is. It reasons from the intellect only. It is not inspired, because inspiration must come from the Spirit within.

11. The Father that dwells within you reveals Himself through your consciousness, because your consciousness is the means through which you express the Father. Be aware in your own consciousness of the great secret of power " I am." Speak the word of power " I am," then your consciousness will realise the tremendous force that is behind it. The Universe is not divided, it is " one " *whole*.

12. Fill the Holy Temple every day with strong assertive vibrations of the Christ Life lifting the atmosphere beyond the mortal senses.

13. Your growth into truth is so simple, so natural, for the Father is working in your midst and cannot fail.

14. You do not live alone. You think that you live by yourself, but that is an illusion of the senses. There is no division in Life, there is no separation between any one of us.

15. There is at the root the one Life, flowing from the one source, the one Spirit manifesting itself in all.

16. If the consciousness in you was in any way separate from the Infinite Consciousness then the Infinite could not be infinite. If you, a living being upon earth, were separate from God, then God could not be Infinite. Now you see clearly that you cannot live alone and that there is no separation anywhere.

17. In the realisation of this truth the symbol used for this pliable substance that fills the whole Universe was known as " water," but in your days other words have

been used for the expression of the same thing, such as electronic substance or ether of space.

18. Although you are aware of many scientific developments that take place on the earth plane, yet you will realise that it is only through the knowledge of the Spiritual that you arrive at the secrets of the Universe.

19. If scientists would open their minds fully to the inspiration that comes from the Spirit, great and mighty things could be revealed to them.

20. The day is coming when this will be so, when the world will be better understood in its relation to the Universe as a whole, showing distinctly that the world that you live in is *in* the " whole " Universe. A portion of its electronic substance that makes up all the Universe is moulded into form, but still exists in the one substance and can never be separated from it. Thus within dwells the mighty power, the Spirit of God—the Christ that creates. This is the Life in man. I am Spirit, the Christ of God, the word that was in the beginning.

21. Beware of those who cause divisions contrary to the doctrine which I have taught you. There never has been any division but only in the mind of man, and this division is born of ignorance.

22. Later when you function only from the consciousness of the Spirit, your bodies will be finer and its obedience will be immediate.

23. If you could but realise the importance of these words, that you are Spirit now, you do not have to wait till you leave the body to become Spiritual beings ; you are already Spiritual beings and you were so from the beginning.

24. And if when you call upon the Christ power, and realise the source whence you come, you will bring into operation a power that is beyond the mortal sense.

25. All is known to the Christ but all is not revealed to the consciousness in man until such time as man unfolds,

and then the Spirit within shall reveal Its glory, Its power, Its essence, Its Love, Its Peace. Only through the quietude of the mind does the Truth unfold itself.

26. If you then, being in the mortal sense, become positively spiritual you could assert now your dominion over all things, thus refusing to recognise the suggestions that come from the senses.

27. It was this that I saw so clearly ; I spoke from the Spirit, thereby infusing Life into everything. If you can think with me and feel with me then you will realise what I mean.

28. When you see clearly that the Life, the only " Living Presence " is God Himself, the Almighty, the Almighty in your midst, and when and as you realise this, your consciousness becomes aware of the power within. The consciousness is the means through which the Spirit manifests itself on all planes.

29. When your consciousness becomes " aware " of Life, Life—being the servant of all—shall manifest according to your awareness of It. Your consciousness unfolds through the realisation of the power of the Spirit ; the consciousness then reveals and expresses that which the consciousness is aware of.

30. Feel then in your heart the power of the Spirit. Feel and recognise in your own consciousness the Christ Power that has been given dominion over all things. All power has been given unto me in heaven and on earth.

31. In this way the Christ shall also reign in you, for the Christ is the only begotten son of the Father who rests upon the Father's breast.

32. He is the King in all Kingdoms and has victory in heaven and on earth.

33. Not even a sparrow will fall on the ground without the Father's will ; therefore, fear not ; for I am always with you.

34. How beautiful is this Truth when you recognise it. Not a part of your body can be affected unless there is a change that takes place in the mind.

35. Everything exists in the mind of God, and nothing can exist outside it. Unless you are born again, this time of Spirit and water, you shall never enter the kingdom. This means that unless you recognise the Truth realising the wholeness of Spirit that manifests, you can never enter into the Kingdom of the Creative Power of the Christ.

36. Everything has been delivered to me by my Father, and no one knoweth the Son except the Father, and no one knoweth the Father but the Son.

37. Then come unto me all you who are tired, all who are carrying burdens, and I will give you rest. This is true, for I am he who shall carry your burden ; if you will but cast that burden upon me, I will lift it from you and you shall be free.

38. The Christ has been given all power in heaven and on earth. Seek ye first the Kingdom of God and His righteousness, and all things shall be added unto you. Seek ye the kingdom of the Spirit and the right use of It, and all shall be added unto you.

39. Your rest is sure, your strength will be fortified by the presence of the Lord thy God.

40. Therefore learn from me, for I am quiet in my heart and strong in my knowing. You will find me a rest to your souls. For your heart is not troubled when you are strong in your knowing of me.

41. Your heart is at peace, full of compassion and love, when you are strong in Christ. Then know the Father as I know Him ; I have personified Him, all His love, all His glory, His compassion, His wisdom, and His power. This knowing in my consciousness reveals the Truth to all men.

42. Everything has been told to me by my Father, and no one knoweth the son except the Father, nor does anyone knoweth the Father except the son. Then come unto me and I will give you rest.

43. My yoke is very pleasant and my burden is light. Think with me in your quiet hours, for I am with you always.

44. Take time off from your daily tasks and go into the quietness and think with me. I am always with you ; you shall feel my presence expressing Itself through you. You will rise comforted, joyful and filled with the " Presence " of the Eternal Christ.

45. Now that you have learned to say " I am Spirit," know that Spirit alone creates.

46. It is the Spirit within you that creates everything. Great is the mighty Mind of God as I know It, yet the senses do not reveal this to you. That which is unseen is more real than that which you see, and from the unseen everything you see has come. The Spirit, the Unseen, is the animating power and brings all form into Being. Spirit makes things by becoming the things It makes. Spirit is complete in Itself. Spirit is all, and all is Spirit.

47. One part of the Spirit cannot be separated from another ; the Spirit manifesting is not separated from Spirit unmanifest. The Life in you is in no way separated from the Life of God.

48. The race is in its childhood in regard to this knowledge, yet many are beginning to feel the urge of the one Life " I am."

49. These words of mine are for the purpose of unfolding the Real behind the shadow, and what I feel you shall also feel as you listen to me : Thus you will learn of me. Study these words until you feel the " knowing."

50. There is what we call telepathic communication from one mind to another or from one consciousness to

another ; there is a direct line of communication just as you have in your world when you take up the instrument you use to hear one person speaking to another from a distance.

51. It is the same here : as above, so below. There is a telepathic communication from one mind to another. The mind that is trained for the work will express the thoughts that I give.

52. You will notice that the consciousness of the brother is raised above the mortal sense, raised above the physical sense, to the consciousness of the inner realm. His consciousness is linked up with the consciousness and then transferred back into the body, using the brain and body as a sounding board.

53. While this process is going on he knows everything that is taking place, but, when transmission by my overshadowing ceases, he knows nothing of what has taken place until such time as he hears it again over the recorder which has been placed at the back of the structure behind him.

54. If the brother would meditate, sit quietly, and enter again into the inner realms of his own consciousness, he would find all imprinted there, and all I have given can be brought forth again. That is why, after these lectures have been given, he will be a greater instrument than ever before to express the Truth.

55. He has been trained in the Himalayas for this purpose—sometimes seven days and longer in complete meditation, without even food or drink, until such time as he was capable of receiving the higher vibration.

56. Consequently we have used him all over the world and we will use him again in different parts of the world. I am telling you these things because you should know them. One day we will take him away from your sight to our world in the Spirit, where he will work again

amongst you invisibly. We have kept him alive, young, strong, virile, and will continue to do so while he is on earth.

57. The finest music you could ever hear on earth can only give you some idea of the beauty beheld in the soul of the composer.

58. So it is with you. What I give you, enables you to feel something of the beauty that is in store for those who love me, and those who love me love my Father also. For I have personified the Father, so that if you know me so you shall also know my Father—your Father.

59. His love flows out as music in the spheres and is caught up in all souls who open up to It.

60. Everyone is seeking happiness, but no one can find it in the outer ; only through the inner realisation can the joyous power of this rhythm be felt.

61. The music, the love, and wisdom of God expresses itself through the soul. Thus you become conscious of It manifesting in your bodies. That is why I say my peace and my love I bring with me, and my peace and my love I leave with you.

62. How can I explain that which is beyond your comprehension ? Only open up yourselves to me and my thoughts will manifest in you.

63. The Father is ever beyond the highest ideal, and your growth reveals more of Him who is the breath of Life.

64. Although the mists are deep upon the earth surface, the light is beginning to pierce its way through, and in your generation many more are beginning to see and to know the Truth.

65. For at present you see dimly through the mist, and only know in part, but you shall know even as you are known.

66. The most of ignorance that I came to pierce 2,000

years ago still remains.   There has been little change in the orthodox religions.

67. So many divisions have been created by the different religions, so much strife.   But, as you now see, there can be no division in God, there can be no division anywhere.

68. Division is born of ignorance in the mind of man. Can this ignorance then be dissolved away ? Yes. Spiritual influences now bearing upon the earth plane are beginning to dissolve this mist of ignorance away, and you and many more like you are the means through which it will be dissolved.

69. Your realisation of this truth in your silent hours will charge the atmosphere with wisdom and love. Your love and peace will help the world.

70. For the Father becomes more lovely as your vision clears ; and what the inner eye sees, so does the soul show forth.

71. This calls you onwards on a never-ending stream of light to the source from which it comes.

72. And His greatness is never greater than when we see Him in His lowliness, where He lifts all to safety through His supreme Love.

73. I gave a parable nearly 2,000 years ago. It is called the Prodigal Son, and if you read that parable again you will see the depth of the Father's Love.

74. No one can ever be separated from the Father, not even His most disobedient child, and that child requires more love than the one who is obedient.

75. This fills the soul with the adoration for His benign Love. For our God is above all gods created in man's mind. For our Father-Mother-God is beyond the greatest conception capable by man.

76. But we will see with open minds the glory of our Father-Mother-God, and with this you shall be transformed

into the same likeness—from one glory to another, just as the Spirit of the Christ, the Son revealing the Father.

77. It is the Christ the Son that recognises the Father. The Christ is the Spirit in you also, and, if you can realise and recognise It, so shall It do for you what It did for me, and if you believe in me you will do greater things. For I am the Christ revealing the Father unto you.

78. It was this that my Blessed Mother saw, and through her vision I was born in the flesh. " I am " the word that became flesh.

79. Your mother on earth is near and dear to God and to yourselves. Try to imagine what joy her sacrifices for you gives her.

80. The nearer you get to mother's love the nearer do you get to the Love of the Father who is manifesting in His creation.

81. For in the mother is seen the Father at work in the forming of His image and likeness. Thus I was born in flesh. " I am the Life."

82. And no one is born in the flesh excepting the Father knoweth, and no one leaves the flesh except the Father also knoweth.

83. Even a sparrow does not fall to the ground except through the will of the Father, neither are you born into the flesh except through the will of the Father.

84. The Father manifesting creates in the mother the image and likeness of Himself. How wonderful it is for you to understand, to know this Truth, that you are the image and likeness of your Father in heaven and within you dwells His Love and Power, His Peace, His Glory.

85. All you who are here in Spirit—I am speaking to you as well. The more you realise this Truth, so shall you give expression to my thought.

86. Let us come before Him with thanksgiving. The

depths of the Earth lie in His hand. The mountain peaks are His ; He made the sea, and He made the land.

87. Let us worship Him in His greatness, bowing before Him Who made us in His own image and likeness.

88. Oh, would the world listen to my voice to-day. " Praise the Eternal, O families of nations, Praise the Eternal for His glory and compassion."

89. Enter His House with an offering of peace and goodwill to all men, and He will rule the nations justly.

90. Let the skies be glad, let the earth rejoice, let the sea thunder its praise. Let the land give forth its fruits in praise, and the trees of the forest sing for joy.

91. The Eternal is present, for He comes with His son to rule the earth, to rule the world justly and the Nations faithfully. That is the promise, and this promise is being fulfilled. The way is being prepared now.

92. The Spirit in man claims its freedom. No longer can it be downtrodden, for the Kingdom of Heaven is at hand : the Kingdom of the inner, the Kingdom of the higher consciousness ; the will of God in heaven shall be done on earth.

93. What is seen in your midst is but the prelude to the Kingdom of Heaven on earth ; the Kingdom of the inner becomes the Kingdom of the outer, and all strife shall pass away.

94. The world like a babe is crying in the night, and with no language, but that cry was answered by the Eternal Father. The world has no language, the world has no truth, the mortal sense shall die, the truth of the living God shall be proclaimed.

95. The world is crying out in its ignorance with no language, as a child cries in the night, yet the mother hears the cries of her babe and rushes to help it ; so has the Father heard the sound, the cry of His children upon earth.

96. I am not blind to your miseries ; I know and understand them ; I have passed through them. You are born in ignorance through belief in separation and division.

97. Think for yourselves now, and you will see how you can be free. By recognising that which is utterly false and untrue, you will know that which is true.

98. I have come that ye shall have life and more abundant life.

99. I have revealed God according to your needs, and the Father is willing to help you according to your needs.

100. Did I not reveal the Father, the hidden Spring, abundant and overflowing, the never-ceasing Life in all its fulness, that you may also rest in the Truth. Then follow in my footsteps because I know the way.

101. There is no mystery in this. No man has ever seen God, but the first-born of God, Who is in the bosom of the Father, he has declared Him.

102. These words mystify those who do not understand them, but as you recognise that the Father Himself gives birth to the Son the Christ which is the image and likeness of the Father Himself, and as the Christ knoweth Himself, so he reveals the Father in all His glory and power, wisdom and love.

103. This is the full rich glorious Life in you and should fill your soul and body. For Christ is your Life.

104. I did not draw down Life from outside God, for I know that I am the eternal Christ of God that lives in every soul.

105. The meaning of my words can be recognised only from within yourselves and not from without.

106. That is why I speak in the way I do, so that within yourselves you will feel the meaning of my words. You cannot explain what I tell you because you can never explain the Truth.

107. Some people will ask, " What did he say ? " " How did he say it ? " But can you tell what I said and how I said it ? Can you explain the Truth ? That which can be explained is not the Truth, but, as you listen to me, so shall you feel the Truth, and only unto those who will listen can it be revealed. You shall feel me and know me, for " I am the Truth."

108. Do not reason with your intellect, for it is limited in its nature and judges from without. The Spirit will reveal all things to you through inspiration.

109. Know that I live in you and that humanity is God's eternal Son. The sheep know their Shepherd's voice.

110. And humanity will say one day, " It is finished," and they shall be one for I shall be in their midst. The Father will glorify Himself in His son, and all humanity will know me.

111. Think what this means, that all humanity will know the love, the wisdom, the compassion, the power of the Christ.

112. The Father will glorify Himself, will express Himself in the Son, the will of God that is done in heaven will be done on earth.

113. Our Father who art in heaven, hallowed be Thy name, Thy Kingdom come, Thy Will be done on earth as it is in heaven.

114. You are my friends because everything that I heard from my Father I make known to you ; thus I chose you to go and produce fruit, and that your fruit might remain—and whatever you ask my Father in my name He will give it to you.

115. Therefore I command you that you love one another. For only in loving one another can I remain in your midst, and where I am, there the Father is also, for I have personified the Father, and the Father is personified in me.

116. You will see me again and your heart will rejoice, and your joy no man will take away from you ; what I have given you, will remain with you.

117. I am not alone, because the Father is forever with me, and when you have seen me you have seen the Father. Can you realise this mighty Truth ? When you have seen me you have seen the Father ; the Father has created me and He remains in me and I remain in Him.

118. I could not come into being except the Father were with me, it is the Father, who ever remaineth within me, He is speaking for me.

119. Eternal Loving Father, I have made Your Name known to those whom You gave me out of the world, they were Yours and You gave them to me, and they shall keep Thy word, the word of the Christ that dwells within them ; because they have heard It, they know It, and now It shall dwell in their souls.

(THE SCRIBE'S REMARKS :

A complete silence spread over the assembly, a bright light shone, and the Master's face appeared completely overshadowing the brother's face.)

120. They know that whatever You have given me is from You.

121. And everything that is mine is Yours and what is Yours is mine and I am glorified by Thee.

122. As I was unchanged by the experience called death, for Life is not divided, there is no division in Life and there is no interruption in the Life by the so-called death.

123. Life is never interrupted, nor is it destroyed or interfered with. It was this that I showed so prominently to my disciples, this I also show to you.

124. Life does not die, and " I am " is unchanged by

the experience of so-called death ; so shall the Spirit, the Life in you, remain unchanged. For you have always been, and cannot die, and as " I am " so shall ye be also, for the Spirit of the Father who raised me from the " dead " dwells within you also.

MY PEACE AND MY LOVE I LEAVE WITH YOU

SILENCE

(THE SCRIBE'S REMARKS :

A Light now enveloped the Brother. So bright is this Light that it fills the hall with a radiance beyond any explanation.)

TALK 7

My Words are from Heaven

My peace, my love I bring to you.

1. We will consider together the value of the Scriptures.

2. " The Scriptures " is a statement of Law of that which is in the realm of Heaven as well as that which is in the realm of earth.

3. The words written in the many books are words of inspiration by the prophets of the Israelites. These prophets were inspired men ; they had made a very deep study of all the things Spiritual.

4. They had the power to bring into operation, through inspiration, knowledge from the Spiritual Source awaiting expression.

5. Most of thse prophets were born for the purpose, and all through the Bible you will read of peculiar things that happened to many of them. Although the words were inspired, nevertheless they were written by men.

6. Inspiration is a power that comes from the Spirit and, as It expresses Itself through Its channel, It is often moulded according to the particular nature of the instrument. There is a purer form of inspiration that comes from the Spiritual Source such as what is happening at this moment, when the consciousness of the Spiritual Power dwelling in the inner realm is manifesting through the inner consciousness of the instrument that is used. In some cases this was also used by those prophets which you read of in the Bible.

7. We call it a book of inspiration and this is the secret of its great value in the world.

8. The soul is always looking for the source of its being,

and this desire leads one to the truth through inspiration. No call goes out from any soul that is not answered from the Spiritual realm.

9. You are all eternally linked-in to the great Almighty Father ; there is no distance between you and the Father, neither is there any distance between you and me. There is no division anywhere ; division and separation iş but a concept of ignorance born in the mind of man.

10. In reality there is no separation ; there is no separation between the Spirit of God in each and every one of you, and the Spirit that is in me and that Spirit is the Spirit of the Father speaking to you ; the Spirit alone has voice.

11. Books, words, letters, are all of no value in themselves ; they have value only when the Spirit uses words as a means of connecting thought to the invisible, thus piercing through the realm of the senses.

12. Thus the word is but the outer shell hiding the pearl of great price which you find within. When you take a word in your own mind and say for instance the words " I am," " I am the Life," these are words expressed through the mortal sense, yet these words can be risen to the Spiritual state which is eternal and ever-present.

13. Thus in reading the Bible, which you call Holy, you will be able to use the words and raise them, although seen through mortal eyes, read through mortal mind, yet, by the power of the Spirit that is inherent in you, you will raise them to a Spiritual level beyond mortal comprehension.

14. The Scriptures have been written through inspiration by guidance of the Spirit for the purpose of instruction in the Law of Life and for the right use of that Law.

15. Therefore I did not come to destroy the Law but to fulfil the Law, to make Life full, to show it manifesting in the human flesh, to prove that the Christ could manifest

in the flesh the glory of the Infinite Father that was living in and expressing Himself through the Son.

16. The Father who had life in Himself expressed that same Life through the Son; therefore the Son expresses the Life, the Will of the Father.

17. My word is quick and powerful, yet it is sweeter than honey.

18. The word the Father gives me is the living word of His Love beyond human comprehension; and His word is a living power, for His Love is always present.

19. When any one of you can feel the power of the Spirit and recognise it completely, and by it speak, then the word you speak has power. All power has been given unto me in heaven and on earth.

20. There are no creations hidden from His light, for all things are naked and open before His eyes.

21. My words are from heaven, the inspiration of the " one " Spirit of God pouring out the abundant wealth and wisdom of God.

22. It is through these words that you also can be inspired, because my words are from heaven, from the inner, the higher consciousness, that realm which the outer never touches. But that realm can express itself outwardly through the outer ; then the outer becomes as the inner.

23. These words are being recorded and transcribed for you, so that in your quiet moment you will be able to absorb them, meditate upon them, thereby making them your own. And by raising them beyond the mortal sense you gain a power and understanding you did not possess before.

24. Inspiration is possible to all; even now you are being inspired to understand the hidden mysteries of life through my words.

25. Therefore my words become the vehicle through

which you learn of the great and glorious truth hidden within you.

26. The miracle of the spoken word is the genius of God who speaks the language of time through mortal sense, yet makes it eternal and spiritual.

27. It is the Father who speaketh in me. It is the Father who speaketh through the mortal sense, through mortal flesh, making these words an eternal and ever-present Reality.

28. Those who are now in the realms of the inner, who have already passed from the mortal flesh, still live ; they also hear my words and are inspired by them.

29. Every one of you can now enter into the higher realms of consciousness beyond the mortal sense through understanding.

30. When I took the word " bread " I gave it a holy and Spiritual meaning to convey the truth of the Spiritual nourishment that shall sustain you in everything.

31. At all times learn to bring the light of Reality and truth into limitation, chaos and darkness, and these shall disappear.

32. Your Creative Power is the consciousness of the Christ in you, and through this consciousness the Christ shall manifest through you to make all things anew.

33. To comprehend my words, you must raise your consciousness beyond the mortal sense, into the realms of Spirit ; then you will understand my words, for they live beyond the mortal sense.

34. You will know the Christ to be the only Eternal Son of God. The Spirit that gives you life, the Spirit that liveth in you is the Spirit that speaketh in me, for the Spirit alone has the power to speak.

35. The consciousness of this Christ is the power in all creation, and the more conscious you are of It so shall It manifest all the greater in your own lives.

36. You thus produce in the outer by the Spirit of the Father. There is no other source of power, there is no other power in the Universe.

37. As I have told you, there is no division anywhere ; God is not divided, neither has He divided Himself ; but in Him, by Him, and with Him, everything that is made is made.

38. Words are but symbols of communication ; but when the Spirit of the Father comes into the outer, there are no words to explain this great illumination.

39. When the outer consciousness becomes aware of the Father, the realm of God will manifest in the outer. It was this that filled my own consciousness when I spoke the " word," and that word was made manifest.

40. Thus it is the same with you if you will but believe. Raise your consciousness above the mortal sense into the Spiritual state by understanding, and there receive the power of the Father through your own consciousness, revealing the mighty power that reigns forever.

41. Have I not proved that the Son of God has all power in heaven and on earth ? This same Spirit that raised me from the dead dwelleth within you also, and will raise you as it did me.

42. This will be your experience as it was mine, and for this I have come to help you.

43. The words I speak and the thoughts of my heart please the Father in regard to you :

44. That you may become the highest expression of my Father moving through all Life, radiating light, manifesting a deep inmost peace, thereby unconsciously manifesting Divinity.

45. And this inward peace is a recognition of great humility, yet this humility, in its magnificence, is " I of my own self can do nothing, it is the Father who ever remaineth within me, He does the work."

46. In this way you unconsciously express Divinity ; wherever you move, whatever you say, whatever you do, you will be expressing Divinity unconsciously so that others are helped by your words and actions.

47. This light cannot be hid, for Love and Wisdom are conveyed in every gesture, in every spoken word. Thus you become an inspired soul.

48. The real value of the word of the Scriptures is to open your understanding to the gifts of God ; and these are bestowed upon you according to your unfoldment.

49. The word " believe " has been wrongly interpreted in the Scriptures. The word " believe " means a deep knowing and it is this deep knowing that gives understanding. And as understanding becomes deeper you become more conscious of the Father who will work through you. Unfold naturally the gifts He has bestowed upon you—they are awaiting your recognition now. Inspiration enables you to unfold your Divine gifts.

50. The inspired writings of the Scriptures have been placed above all books, and millions have been inspired and raised by the word of Truth.

51. This is the Law of Transmutation working in you, and, through my words to you, you transmute the lower into the higher.

52. Think what happens to you during my talks with you : every experience in your life is lifted into the highest and thereby purified.

53. When I speak to you, everything that has happened in your lives is raised to that state where it is purified. All the dross is dissolved away because the Spirit alone retaineth the essence. The perfect Creative Force—the Spirit of God—creates in Its own Eternal substance wherein there is no division.

54. Spirit is consciousness, and consciousness acts on this substance by means of Its intelligent action. The

consciousness and the Intelligence of God manifests through all Life.

55. In this inseparable, in this indivisible, mind of God all things are created and nothing is apart from Him. Therefore in truth, in Reality, all is perfect.

56. As these words of mine raise you to that state of understanding, so every experience in your life is raised up by that understanding.

57. This key I will put into your hand. Seek the Spirit, not the letter, and, as you wait, I will unfold the truth in you.

58. The Christ is the conqueror in all things, for the Christ is the Spirit of God individualised in you. Seek the Spirit behind the word and it will manifest in your life.

59. When you read the Scriptures or any inspired work, and especially these words that I have given for the purpose of your meditation, seek the Spirit behind the word. It is not the letter or the word you must seek, but wait upon it, think deeply, and I will inspire you, I will express the Truth of it in you.

60. By this way you shall make it your own, and only in this way can the Truth be revealed in you. It must come from within and not from without. These words will raise your consciousness into that realm of Spirit where all is understood.

61. It is written in the Scriptures that the Spirit of God descended like a dove and spoke these words, "This is my beloved Son with whom I am well pleased."

62. Direct voice has often been heard from the unseen and this was not unknown amongst those who understood the Law in my time on earth. It was used even more then than now.

63. Many of you, I know, are not yet familiar with a direct voice from heaven. It is only in that particular quietude of the mind where there is silence that it is

heard, and this is most effectively obtained in the Himalayas of the mind.

64. This same Spirit which manifested then is manifesting now in your midst.

65. And this same Spirit will minister unto you if you will but believe it.

66. Do you understand what I mean now, that the power of my thought moving in your consciousness reveals the Truth ? Truly I tell you that the last moment is the greatest when sustained by faith, for in it is seen the glorious power of the Spirit.

67. It was in this last moment that Peter failed to sustain himself on the waves.

68. This story has been written in many languages and in many ways, the true facts being as follows :

69. The power to walk upon the water is inherent in all if you had the understanding and faith to accomplish it.

70. When you try to swim at first you lose your faith and you begin to flounder. As you become more confident in yourself you are able to sustain yourself on the surface of the water. It requires a greater amount of faith and understanding to walk upon the water, yet this is possible.

71. It was John who first noticed my form walking on the waves.

72. The impetuous Peter standing in their midst exclaimed : " My Lord, my lord, if this be truly you, bid me come to you on the waves." And I bade him come.

73. When Peter stepped upon the waves they were as solid as a rock to him and he walked. Peter at that moment was filled with the Power of the Spirit. His desire was to walk on the waves and come to me and do exactly what I was doing.

74. Impetuous Peter then walked upon the waves but it was not long before he began to think that he had never done this before ; it was something new, something strange to him.

75. He walked until he thought within himself what would happen if the waves would break under him—he would sink.

76. Then the waves did break and he began to sink. Fear had overtaken him.

77. I said to him, " O Peter, why did you doubt ? "

78. I want to ask you that same question. Why do you doubt ? Then ask yourselves this question : " Why *do* you doubt when you understand now that the Spirit of God dwells in you and that the Christ has all power in heaven and on earth and has dominion over all things ? "

79. Ask yourself again the question : Why *do* you doubt ? Is it lack of understanding ? Or is it fear of something that is unfamiliar, that which you do not understand you become afraid of ?

80. Thank Thee, Father, Thou hast shown me that there is nothing unfamiliar between Thee and me, for we are *one*.

81. Is this not true also in your lives on earth ? You do not understand the power of the Spirit, you are blinded by the fear of the unusual.

82. The food that one eats to nourish the flesh soon passes away. You must seek the food that feeds the soul and this is the Bread from heaven.

83. This is the Christ ; I am the Bread from heaven that God has given unto the world. Therefore you must eat of me.

84. They who eat this Bread from heaven and drink from the Spring of Life shall live for ever and shall be exalted to the throne of power.

85. I am the Bread from heaven, the Bread of the Father who sent me. The Father is Love, and Wisdom and nothing is kept from me. I only ask and He shows me, and what I see the Father do I do likewise.

86. Seek ye first the Kingdom of God within and the

right use of that Kingdom, and all else shall be added unto you.

87. The beneficent Law is ever operating in your lives and you have power to help others, only bring them into the light of your own consciousness, raised to the consciousness of the Christ.

88. Every act of your life, every thought, you should lift up into the light ; then there will come into your consciousness the realisation of that Kingdom within, where nothing from without can touch.

89. When you stand in that Kingdom, no matter what storms are raging in the outer, you are safe in the Kingdom, for in It all power is given unto you.

90. When you are in that state of peace, in the mind of God, then there is the Creative Principle that said : " Let there be light, and there was light."

91. This same power is within you. With this awareness, say, " Peace," and the storm shall abate. Say it with understanding. Say it with the power of the Spirit, with the understanding of the Christ, " I am the Life." " My Beloved Father and I are one."

92. You will become one with me, no longer doubting ; you will have begun to be even as your Father in heaven is. Be ye perfect, as your Father in heaven is perfect.

93. As the world unfolds the mysteries of Life, so will I inspire men and women to do even greater things in your day.

94. As the race unfolds, so shall further unfoldings be expressed from the heart of Life. There is a continual unfoldment of Life.

95. The race is moving forward and the inner realms are becoming more unfolded in the outer. Truth is being revealed throughout the Nations.

96. Here and there groups are working, groups who have advanced to that stage where they can understand

the inner realm, enabling them through inspiration to understand the mysteries of life that are hidden within.

97. The masses at present are taken up with division, but you will see that this division is born of ignorance. As I have said before, there are other flocks. I shall go and bring them and they shall be one flock and one shepherd.

98. I want you to open your minds free from divisions, with wider vision day after day, for greater things are coming.

99. What you will learn now, will reveal the old to you again, for I am pointing the way, along which truth can be revealed to you. These instructions are leading you to the power of the Christ.

100. To be born of the Spirit is to know and recognise the Truth that you are born of the Spirit, that you are Spirit ; and because you are Spirit now, so shall you always be Spirit, and it is the Spirit of God that is born in you. This is the power hidden within, " Unless you are born from above. . . ."

101. Truly I tell you, no one can see the realm of God unless he is born from above.

102. For what is born of Spirit is Spirit ; the inherent Life is the real and only power.

103. You enter into your highest riches through your realisation of your oneness with me in the Father, as I am one with Him from the beginning.

104. Perhaps it is difficult through your mortal sense to understand this, but " I am the Truth," and if you will open your mind, my telepathic thought will raise your consciousness into the realm of that which had no beginning. And that which had no beginning must exist eternally ; then the Spirit of God, the Spirit of the Father existing in you, is eternal and ever-present.

105. When you recognise this Truth your vision ex-

pands. There is no longer any division. There is no longer any limitation. These limitations dissolve away and leave you complete and perfect in the mind of God as He holds you. The Father created you in His own image and likeness.

106. The Christ within you is the same yesterday, to-day, and forever. Wait in silence that I may speak in you, write through you, my thoughts, my designs, my purpose expressed through you.

107. Do not be carried away by different doctrines, but let my words linger in your souls until you feel the thrill of life, the upspringing of the eternal Son of God.

108. If you live in separation from one another, you cannot live completely in the Father.

109. You must see that there is no division, you must see that there is no separation anywhere—this is the almighty Truth. This is the truth that gives me power in heaven and on earth, and it will give you the same.

110. I am one with Thee, Loving Father, to know that I am Thy son, born of Thee, inherent within me Thy Wisdom, Thy Love and Thy Power. This inheritance Thou hast given to me as Thy beloved Son with whom Thou art well pleased.

111. Be at peace, all those who carry burdens ; listen to me, my voice will lead you, my strength will support you, and my love will remain with you always.

112. Then your light shall shine before the world so that the world shall see your good works and glorify your Father in heaven.

113. I did not come to weaken the Law of the Prophets, for I am the fulfilment of the Law, and not one jot or tittle shall pass from the Law, till all be fulfilled, for through me the Law of God is made manifest in the world.

114 I want you to think deeply on this. Lift it to the inner consciousness and there dwell upon it.

115. Let the Spirit of Christ within you be your only guide. It is for this purpose that I have come that you may know yourselves now.

116. My love for you is very great ; therefore, let my love live in you. For love is all Power in heaven and on earth.

117. It is the Spirit of God that dwelleth in me and speaketh for me. And I also speak for you and whatsoever you ask remembering me, so shall I ask the Father who shall give unto you whatever you ask remembering me.

118. By remembering me, you know the Love of God, the Wisdom of God and the power of God and you know that this dwells within yourselves, not as something relative apart from you, but a Reality which is the Real You.

119. Remember me and I shall come to you and you shall know me. In nowise shall I turn my face from anyone, only be at peace and remember me.

120. It is impossible for the mind of man to affect the Spirit in any way ; then always lean on the Spirit, for it is all-power ; the Christ of God is your only Reality.

MY PEACE AND MY LOVE I LEAVE WITH YOU TO REMAIN WITH YOU

We will now take the Sanctuary hour. Do not close your eyes but look towards me.

SILENCE

The peace, the love, the wisdom, the healing of God is expressed through you now.

(THE SCRIBE'S REMARKS :

As the Master left, a beautiful aroma of perfume unknown to anyone filled the hall, while music and singing were heard.)

TALK 8

THE KINGDOM OF HEAVEN IS WITHIN

My peace and my love I bring to you.   My peace and my love
remain with you.

" The Kingdom of Heaven is within you "

1. Heaven is the Kingdom of the innermost or Spiritual, otherwise called the Christ Consciousness, the tabernacle of the Most High.

2. Earth is the symbol of the outer or opposite or material, both eternally subsisting in the " One " in perfect unity.

3. The Kingdom of Heaven is within you. This statement has been proclaimed all over the world, but few have understood the deeper meaning of it.

4. When you realise the deeper meaning of this saying of mine, then you will realise also the power that goes with it, for in the inner realms there dwells the Most High.

5. God the Almighty in your midst is strong, He falters not. He is greater than the greatest, He is beyond the comprehension of even the Archangels, yet He dwells in you and His dwelling place is called the Kingdom of Heaven within you

6. When this is misunderstood or not recognised, mankind creates his own hell.

7. When you realise and recognise this wonderful truth you are no longer separated or alone. There is a feeling of unity, there is a feeling of oneness that remains permanent and everlasting to the individual who recognises it.

8. This recognition comes through understanding, sometimes through meditation, but never through separation or division.

9. It can never be yours completely if you are separated from one another in any way whatsoever, because when you seek deep in yourselves there you shall find me knocking at the door of your hearts waiting to enter in, and in every soul this is taking place.

10. Those who have admitted me into their hearts must admit everyone, no matter how difficult that person may be, no matter how evil that person may seem ; they are all admitted within the one heart of Christ, and no one is ever cast out who comes unto me.

11. Freedom comes when the Kingdom of Heaven is recognised as the true state of man's consciousness, the true expression of the Father ; I and the Father are one.

12. If you then can comprehend the deeper meaning of this saying, " I and the Father are one," and you actually know it to be true, and as you repeat it to yourself, the outer self will change ; because whatever the inner knows and understands, so shall the outer manifest.

13. It is this mighty power that I understand and feel. This is my recognition and realisation of the Truth. It is the Father who ever remaineth within me and He is working in me. It is He who is performing His own deeds.

14. The Spirit of the Eternal, the Christ of God, preceded all creation—" I am before Abraham," recognising that " I am " is the Life, not only in Abraham but in every living soul.

15. It was this clear statement that I made to bring home the truth to the world, to show definitely that the Christ of God was in the beginning, " I am before Abraham."

16. The world recognised its prophets who were already dead ; at the same time they disregarded the Truth of the Everlasting Life : but when the Christ was raised from the Cross, then the task was fulfilled.

17. Heaven and earth is the operation of the " one " Eternal Spirit expressing Itself in form, yet there is no

separation. The body is but the focal point through which the invisible man functions.

18. The Christ of God, to manifest, is involved in the form created, and existing in the " one " and the One existing in all.

19. Life alone lives, and this is the all-important truth. " Truth " has no beginning, therefore there is nothing new ; all that is to be, is already known to God.

20. The fact that you are here is by no mere chance, the fact that you are here was already known to God. Even a sparrow does not fall to the ground lest the Father knoweth, even the hâirs of your head are numbered.

21. In this recognition there is an intelligence that is active everywhere, and this Intelligence expresses itself through the Consciousness that becomes aware of It. The greater the awareness, the greater the manifestation of The Intelligence.

22. This Intelligence is active and never passive. It is continually outpicturing the desires of the Spirit, for within you the Christ dwells and is the only Creative Power in you.

23. The root of all your misery lies in the conception of being separate from Truth or Life; this is why I said, " I am the Life." " The Father and I are one."

24. You cannot see Truth, yet Truth unfolds in you from the Kingdom of Heaven within.

25. This is your safeguard against false teachers. Let the Spirit within be your guide. This is the reason I have come to reveal the Kingdom of Heaven that is within you.

26. When you begin to understand that the Christ of God dwells within you, you will not look outside for Him. You will be guided and directed to understand by those who have already found Him. And by following in the footsteps I have laid for you, then you shall find The Christ, the same Christ that spoke through Jesus.

27. When there is perfect unity between all of you, you can do great things for the world and for all who live in it, for there I am in the midst.

28. There must be silence in the outer when the Christ of God speaks from the inner. The mortal sense reacts to things external to the self. The roaring noise coming from the external must not affect the consciousness of the Christ within.

29. Your consciousness becomes troubled through misunderstanding the Truth. But immediately you begin to know the Truth that the Christ is all-supreme, then there is a calmness within, and the outer becomes calm also. My peace I bring to you.

30. You can feel my peace in your soul. Then let the Christ speak in all his power and glory with the understanding that it is the Father who ever remaineth with me and you. It is He Who is speaking to you through me.

31. The great works of healing can be done only when the mortal senses have ceased to be and the consciousness turned towards the Kingdom of Heaven within.

32. This is the water I give to you, that you may never thirst again, for it will become a well of living water springing up to Life Everlasting.

33. I speak of that which I have seen with my Father, and, as God is my Father and your Father also, so must you love one another as I love you.

34. When you turn your thoughts and your hearts inwardly, your soul begins to feel the warmth of the Christ of God, the only begotten Son of God who is and was with God from the beginning. Nothing came into being except by Him, and through Him all that is made is made.

35. When you see the beauty of the love of the Father expressing Itself through the Son, then you will know that the Son is the Love of God.

36. The Son knows and understands that this love is pouring continuously through him, and, as the Son receives it, so he expresses it naturally. That is why you must love one another as I love you.

37. No greater thing can you do but to love one another and keep to my sayings, for I speak the truth the Father gives me, and this truth shall set you free.

38. Sin is the great falseness connected with your outer self of the senses ; it belongs to separation and chaos.

39. I have told you not to gaze too long upon the sin of the world which so many are preaching about. How can you see the Christ if you are forever gazing at sin ?

40. When you look to the Christ in yourself, this separateness, this chaos, this sin, that exists in your mind and heart shall dissolve away.

41. Heed not then those who try to drag you through hell, but listen to those who lift you into the glory of the Christ that dwells within you. The Kingdom of Heaven is His dwelling place and His Kingdom is within you now.

42. Many who have passed beyond the flesh know well that flesh and blood does not enter into the higher realms, yet they now know that they are the same who lived in the flesh.

43. Christ dwells in you, and, as you unfold into your higher understanding, so shall this Christ manifest in His glory according to your understanding.

44. When you consciously know yourselves as you are known, you will say in your hearts: " It is finished." Yet separateness and chaos have dared to set up their kingdom of darkness in your midst.

45. I am the Light of the World ; this all-prevailing inner light becomes visible as your inner vision of the Kingdom of Heaven is developed.

46. The inner becomes the outer and the outer becomes

the inner, and as you feel in your heart so it shall be expressed outwardly.

47. It is the word that lives in your heart that manifests. Then seek ye first the Kingdom of Heaven and all other things shall be added unto you. Seek first this mighty Power of the consciousness of God so that it becomes your consciousness. God being Infinite, there can only be " one " consciousness, the Consciousness of God manifesting as the Christ in you.

48. Learn to become conscious of the Father who ever remains in you, and that there is nothing impossible with the Father ; and whatever you shall say, so it shall be done.

49. This is the Light that existed in the beginning before the world was, for I was with God when He said, " Let there be Light " and there was Light and this is the Light that lighteth every soul that comes into the world.

50. Everything that exists must be an expression from the inner, for everything that is made exists only because of the Christ that existed from the beginning.

51. In God, the only " one " subsisting Being, all things must take place, for there is nothing outside Him being Infinite in Nature.

52. If you then know that Life is God and God is Life, and you become aware of this Living Life as yourself, then you will know the Christ of God.

53. O Mighty Wonderful Father, it is a pleasure and a joy to exist in Thee and to know It is Thee who alone exists in us all.

54. How wonderful is the joy in my heart knowing that Thou hast given me all those who belong to Thee, and when they know me I shall give them back to Thee, and I shall still be in their midst, for Thou who speaketh through me shall also speak through them, for no one exists besides Thee.

55. Thus the Creation of the inner and the outer, the active and the passive principles spoken of as Heaven and Earth, are within Him, the only " One."

56. Therefore the only Creative Power you have must come from the Kingdom of Heaven, the inner, the active living Presence expressing Itself in the outer.

57. When you enter into the Kingdom of your own consciousness you will realise where the Christ dwells, and you will know the Creative Power of the Christ.

58. By knowing that God is Love, His son must be Love also. Therefore you reveal the perfectness of the Father through the realisation of His Divine Love, which remains always a protection for yourselves and others.

59. If then you know me and heed my word ye shall create in the outer that which is perfect within you. Be ye perfect as your Father in heaven is perfect.

60. How consciously real is this inner realm to me, you will not fully understand until you come into the inner.

61. You have seen me overshadowing the brother, some of you have seen the power radiating from the heart, some of you have seen many other wonderful things, but even these things are but nothing compared to the Divine Presence that lives within yourselevs.

62. How consciously real is this inner realm to me, so it shall be to you also, for where I am, there also shall you be.

63. This inward self—the Christ—is greater than you can ever realise, for all things are under his control.

64. The Christ Life in you is ever re-creating within, making things anew, bringing the soul into unity with the whole.

65. As you begin to feel this unity you begin to feel the love and the power of God. There is an expansiveness that manifests in all, no matter who they may be. In this lies the power of Christ.

66. The Father can only express Himself in His Wholeness in His completeness, then the Christ in you is the expression of the Father.

67. Everything you read in the New Testament has also a symbolic meaning.

68. When I made a whip of cord and drove out of the Temple the money changers, I also upset the trays of money, the symbol of the outer.

69. I charged them not to make the Father's House a house of robbers and thieves.

70. This is symbolic of driving out of the Temple of the Living God the thieves and robbers of mortal sense. For I must possess the living Temple of God completely. This is the right of my possession.

71. It is the thieves and robbers of mortal sense that deprive you of the power that exists within you. A belief in the outer, a belief in the power of something that has no power in itself is the cause of your weakness.

72. You did not create the Christ, but Christ creates in you. You only create in the outer by the power within you. I say unto you, when you have seen me you have seen the Father, and I am within you.

73. I possess the right to occupy the temple of the Living God wholly and solely. There can be no compromise.

74. He that wholly turneth unto me, out of his innermost being shall flow torrents of Living Water.

75. When you turn completely unto me and give yourselves completely over to me, then from your innermost being will flow my Life, my power, my wisdom, my Love. You will be amazed at the things you can do, and nothing will be impossible unto you if you will but believe and understand me.

76. How much do you believe? Even now you are wondering if what I told you is really true !

77. Unless you believe completely and wholly in me as the Christ the only living Son, the only begotten Son of God, the only power existing in the world, you shall have no real power.

78. To him that hath shall be given, but he that hath not, even that which he hath shall be taken away. Heed my words, they are as the double-edged sword.

79. Therefore it is not for you to imitate the ways of the outer world, but to be transformed by the Christ within, that you may discern what is good and acceptable unto the Father, and reject that which is false.

80. Anything that separates you from one another is a falsehood ; separation denies the Christ in you.

81. The Christ is the only creative power in each and every one. It is the Will of the Father, and His Will will be done on earth as it is in heaven.

82. All members of the body have not the same function, yet they are of the one body.

83. So it is with you ; you are many, and you work differently. Yet you are all of one body ; the body of the Christ holds all, and His Spirit is in all. Please think deeply with me.

84. You have all different gifts according to the grace that is given unto you. Some of you may have clear sight, others may have more faith ; some may have the gift of teaching, and some of healing ; some the gift of consoling. Yet it is the one Christ that is manifesting in you all, and you live in the one body of Christ.

85. Whatever you do, do it with sincerity. Be kind and affectionate to one another and show your mercy with cheerfulness, for mercy is a reward of greatness.

86. It shows the Consciousness of the Christ within. It shows that the outer is being influenced by the living Christ that dwells in the kingdom of heaven within.

87. For no matter who they are, whoever comes unto

me I will in no wise cast him out. Listen then to what I have to say unto you; what I do you must do like-wise, otherwise you are no disciple of mine.

88. In business do not be slothful or deceitful, but serving with honour; thus you serve me and you will not then be wise in your own conceits.

89. And live in peace with all whom you serve and with them who serve you.

90. For it is written in the Kingdom of Heaven, He that is greatest is the servant of all. And who is the greatest? It is the Father who ever remaineth within you. It is He who is the servant of all, and whatsoever you ask in my name so the Father shall give unto you.

91. Therefore, if your enemy hunger feed him; if he thirst give him drink; for whatsoever you do unto any-one, so you do unto me.

92. Overcome all evil with good, for whatsoever thou doeth in thine own heart so shall that be done unto you.

93. Do you praise while you despise? Are you kind to some and unkind to others? Would you feed the soul that is antagonistic to you as cheerfully as one in your own family? Whatever you do unto anyone you do unto me. Therefore follow in my footsteps and all power shall be given unto you in heaven and on earth.

94. Whatever the Father seeth me do, so does He bless a hundredfold; I am truly rich because my Father is rich.

95. All belong to the Father, all are His children; He loves everyone, all people, no matter how disobedient they may be.

96. I reign supreme. All that shall tend to destroy the Temple of our Father shall be under my feet.

97. And when all things be subdued by me, so shall I also be subject unto the Father who sent me, for He putteth all things in their right place, so that we may be all " one " in the Father.

98. The Christ is the seed in the natural body, and is raised in a spiritual body. The body is but the focal point through which the Christ works.

99. There is a natural body and a spiritual body, but the Christ is the ruler of both.

100. Adam was made a living soul by the quickening of the Spirit.

101. The outer man is the earth, the inner is the Lord of Heaven, and the Lord of Heaven has control over all things, for all power has been given unto him ; he is the Lord and the Law.

102. The Law is not above the Lord, but the Lord is above the Law. " I am " the Law, saith the Lord.

103. When you recognise this, then you will see with your own eyes the living expression of the Almighty, for He alone through the Christ has created you in His own image and likeness.

104. And within each and every soul dwells the Christ, the one and only Son ; therefore you live in the body of the Christ, and the Christ Spirit lives in each and every one of you.

105. As you are born the image of your Father in Heaven, so is that image reflected in the outer through the Christ in you.

106. The outer is the flesh and blood, yet flesh and blood does not enter the Kingdom of Heaven, for this is the realm of Spirit and water in which the flesh has no say.

107. Water means that invisible substance, the Mind of God in which everything is existing. With this finer substance everything is created, even flesh and bone. The form may disappear, but the Spirit remaineth forever.

108. But as the soul is raised by the power of the Spirit, and is raised beyond the vibrations of the flesh, so It departs into the inner realms, there to abide with me, for

" I am " in the outer while in the inner, yet I am not affected by flesh and blood. I have overcome the world by the power of the Spirit, and the flesh has no say in the matter.

109. The outer is the flesh and blood, yet flesh and blood does not enter the Kingdom of Heaven. Flesh and blood is the means through which the Christ manifests on earth.

110. That which is untrue in the outer shall pass away, because from the heart of love comes the healing of forgiveness.

111. This mighty Love blots out all sin and separateness, for within you dwells him who has overcome sin and death through the Consciousness of the Christ of God.

112. Because you are the sons and daughters of God, He has sent forth the Spirit of the Christ into your hearts crying Abba Avon—O Father, our Father—so you are servants no longer, but sons and daughters, all heirs to all that which is God's through the Christ the only begotten Son of God that dwells within you.

113. Yes, how many thousands of you are listening to me at this moment, living in a state where time and space do not enter in. But here in the outer, where I am speaking to those who are your brothers and sisters, yet remaining in the flesh, they know time and space. Time and space is the difficulty they have to overcome upon the earth. The difficulty all must overcome is the sense of time and space.

114. You still observe distances, days and months, times and years. This is the illusion of time and space.

115. See yourselves in the Kingdom of Heaven ; the same Spirit within you is the same that created the world.

116. When you understand this, you will see beyond the world of time and space.

117. I said that I am not of the outer but born of the Spirit of God the Father. Call no man your father on earth, for one is your Father who is in heaven.

118. I knew of this greater and inner state of being, and that the outer was but the shadow. Therefore I overcame the temptation of the senses through which time and space made for separation.

119. If you overcome this sense of time and space, you shall also enter into this understanding where all is NOW, where there is no separation, no distance, no time.

120. The originating Spirit of the Father, existing in the simple unity with all power, created the active and passive principles spoken of as Heaven and Earth.

121. So the work done in the inner or heaven is reproduced in the outer or earth. Seek ye first the Kingdom of God, and ye shall create in the outer that which is acceptable to Him who created you within Himself, His Spirit the ruling Power in heaven and on earth.

122. The ways of God the Father are perfect, and the soul that is Conscious of the Living Christ is lifted into the simple unity of the Father Who is Eternal and Everpresent.

123. The simple unity ! How gloriously lovely and perfect, how simple is the Truth, how difficult it is for those who dwell in time and space to understand.

124. When the Christ was raised from the Cross the work of redemption was fulfilled, the whole race was lifted up into unity with the Father.

125. The Christ is the Son of God ; this Christ is the Spirit that animates the whole of humanity, and is the Spirit animating you, the highest creation of God on earth, made in God's likeness.

126. The Spirit took upon itself the body of flesh. The Spirit took upon itself the Satan of the senses while

dwelling complete in that everlasting state of Eternal Power.

127. To enter into the body of flesh is to feel the sense of separation, yet the Christ Spirit knew the senses of the mortal flesh for what they were and said, " Get ye behind me, Satan."

128. The Satan of the senses blinds you from the Christ power that you have here and now.

129. Know that when the Christ was raised from the Cross, so was the whole of mankind raised. The acceptance of this Truth and the understanding of it will set you free now.

130. It is of this I have come to show you, to tell you that you are free now, if you will but believe in me and Him Who sent me.

131. Love is pressing through the surrounding atmosphere about you ; this Love is calling for your obedience, to treat one another with the same Spirit as you see me do.

132. Love dwells in every living soul. Love much and I shall do my work through you.

133. How I long to express this feeling of love in you— the Love of God made manifest.

134. The feeling of Love that goes out from the very centre of your soul is but a grain of sand on the seashore of love. But to understand the Love of God, you must begin to love more, and as you love more so I shall work in you, and through you, because I am love, the Son of the Father of Love.

135. I love all in the world. I am with you in the world working to bring the Kingdom of Heaven to earth ; for this I was sent forth to do.

136. Follow me, for indeed you are the Light of the World. Then let your light shine so that all may see your good works and glorify your Father which is in Heaven.

137. The Kingdom of Heaven is within you.

Now let us all enter into the Sanctuary of the Silent Healing Power.

MY PEACE, MY LOVE, OUR FATHER'S LOVE I LEAVE WITH YOU.

(THE SCRIBE'S REMARKS:

A deep silence reigns and many are healed by the glorious presence.)

TALK 9

HE WHO HATH SEEN ME HATH SEEN THE FATHER

My blessings, my peace remain with you all.
He who believes in me believes not in me but Him who sent me.
He who beholds me beholds Him who sent me.

1. These words are significant and they are true, but only those who have gone beyond separation can understand them.

2. He who has seen me has seen the Father. How few people have understood this wonderful expression of Truth. This expression of Truth, when understood, reveals the Father and places that soul beyond the outer darkness that surrounds the individual.

3. The most important thing of all is to recognise that God alone lives and He is expressing Himself now. It is the Father who ever remaineth within me ; it is He who speaketh, it is He who is performing His own deeds ; this you must realise also.

4. It is because I have recognised Him wholly, and allowed nothing to interfere with this realisation, that by Him and through Him I live ; He speaks for me while I reveal Him to you.

5. You are beginning to understand because you have heard me repeat this Truth so many times. Only by repetition will the Truth take root in your mind and grow to maturity.

6. It is by repetition that I am able to give you the Truth you cannot see with your eyes, for only through the inner vision is It revealed.

7. That which is hidden from the outer is not seen with the physical eyes, but only understood through the inner vision that sees the Truth through Inspiration.

8. As the soul is raised, so the Truth, the consciousness of God, reveals Himself as the Spirit that lives in you.

9. The Spirit that animates the body is the only living power there is; there is no other power in heaven or on earth. It is with this recognition that I said all power has been given unto me in heaven and on earth.

10. As your consciousness becomes aware of the eternal unity of the whole in which we all exist, you are able to grasp the mighty power of this saying of mine. He that hath seen me hath seen the Father. Can you understand it now? Is it possible for you now to realise the meaning of it completely? When you have seen me you have seen the Father.

11. As there is no other living being but God, God must fill boundless space to be Infinite; then He must live in me and I must live in Him and He must live in you, and you must live in me and we together are one in Him Who is Infinite.

12. Without these conditions God cannot be Infinite in nature. There is no separation anywhere, and this is the Truth that I tell you now: *he that has seen me has seen the Father.*

13. You are in the Father now, and the Father is in you, and you can enter into this truth consciously as I did, and of this I have come again to tell you, and truly I tell you, " I and the Father are one."

14. These words I am giving you through the brother are being taken down so that you can study them carefully. They are given in such a way as to reveal the inner; the many repetitions are necessary for your understanding.

15. Through your deep contemplation upon them you will be able to realise the inner meaning, and thereby bring the Truth which is the central power in you to the outer, so that in the outer every cell of your body shall proclaim the Truth.

16. Men and women all over the world have made this discovery for themselves and henceforth all is well ; they have ceased to hurry, for the journey is over.

17. When you recognise that you are in the Father's house and that in that house there is plenty for all, you sit at the Father's table and partake of the feast thereof.

18. This then is the secret of true understanding, when the consciousness becomes aware of itself, aware of itself as being the Spirit of God that created all things, and is now manifesting as it was in the beginning and will be forever the same.

19. Now that you have also made this discovery you are no longer strangers in the Father's house, for I am " one " with you in the Father's house and I will testify for you.

20. I am " one " with you ; know ye not that the Christ of God is the only begotten Son of the Father, the only living Spirit of God in heaven and on earth, having consciousness, intelligence, wisdom and love ; all the qualities of the Father are expressed through the Son. As the Father has life in Himself, so He granted the Son to have the same life in himself.

21. I AM the Spirit that dwells in your soul. Know ye not that I am with you ? The recognition of this enables you to reach me at once. Do not pray to someone afar off, for I am nearer than hands or feet.

22. I have said also, whatsoever you ask in my name my Father shall grant you. Know that I am with you, not apart from you ; and in your prayers believe what I say and you will find, what you ask you shall receive believing you have it.

23. You will no longer say, Behold it is here or behold it is there, for you know that the Kingdom of God is within you.

24. You are just where you have always been in your

eternal home, only you were not conscious of it, and there is no separation from those you love.

25. There is no separation in the Spiritual—the real—there is no parting as you feel in the mortal state. In the Spiritual there is a greater unity, revealing more of Reality.

26. In your mortal state there dwells ignorance, and ignorance causes fear to take hold of the soul. The Light that lighteth the world must shine in mortal consciousness; the Light dwells forever in the consciousness that knows Itself to Be.

27. The Father is in the Son, because the Life in the Father and in the Son is the same Life.

28. When I come into your midst I feel your sense of separation, yet I have come to tell you truly that there is no separation, that there is no truth in distance and space.

29. To comprehend this, is the secret of all power invested in the Spirit manifesting in each and every one.

(SCRIBE'S REMARKS: Speaking to the invisible ones.)

30. Many of you who come here to hear the Christ know these disciples of mine who have gathered round me here on earth, they also know that many of you also dwelt upon the earth ; you now know that it is the same Life ; you are not dead as many believed.

31. At one time you dwelt in mortal fear of death, yet you did not die. You are now very much more alive than you have ever been, and you will continue to be more alive as you consciously awaken to the power of the Life of the Christ that dwelleth within each and every one of you.

32. As I told you before, my voice is heard not only upon this plane but is heard also in all the planes of consciousness. Yet it is the one Consciousness manifesting

in all—all linked together in the one whole, for the Spirit the Father is manifesting in all planes.

33. You will see that those who are around me now are just as important although they have not experienced the passing called death ; yet by believing in me and Him who sent me, they have already passed from death to External Life.

34. With this clear understanding you will no longer hold to the false idea of limitation. Behold I am he who lives, who had passed through death, and behold I am alive forever more.

35. Those who believe in the flesh are already dead, but those who truly believe that the Spirit of God dwells within them are in Eternal Life and Peace. This is the Christ who says when you have seen me you have seen the Father.

36. And again I say to you that the Spirit of the Father who raised me from the dead also dwells within you ; and as He raised me, so shall He raise you.

37. You are not indebted to the flesh, but live by the Spirit of God ; therefore ye are the sons and daughters of God.

38. The consciousness of mankind is being stirred, and everywhere the Truth is springing forth like the sap in the tree sending forth life to every limb and branch.

39. This sap of truth that is permeating the whole of humanity is the Truth of the Christ Life existing in every living soul, revealing that there is no separation.

40. The one Fountainhead of Love and Life is responsible for every existing living being in the Universe, and from this source all existence owes its Being.

41. Old bonds are bursting, old dead creeds are falling away ; like branches without sap or Life they cannot remain alive.

42. The whole race is being lifted up to a higher plane of

thought ; I am in your midst filling the void made by useless words and dogmas, so that you no longer cling to that which is false.

43. No longer listen to those who preach a God afar off, but listen to the Spirit that is within you ; there dwells the Truth.

44. If you are bound by the beliefs of others then you *are* bound. I have come to loosen your bonds, to set you free. I set you free by giving you the Truth of the one Living God, the Truth of the Living God that is in you. He alone is living. I am living because He lives, because the Father hath Life in Himself so does He grant the son to have Life in himself.

45. The knowledge of your oneness with God, to be consciously aware of it, is your whole salvation. This is the open door to freedom.

46. Your minds in the past have been crammed with false thinking from the outer, and thus you closed the door to the Divine inner, the only Reality.

47. When you believe what others have said without reason and have accepted their beliefs, you become an imitator and not a thinker, so you are bound.

48. You have no longer any power to think for yourselves when you worship an image, and that which you worship destroys your thinking, because you are lost in ignorance and no longer able to see the Truth of the only " one " Living God who dwells within.

49. Your sense of separation from me, from one another and from God has been your great enemy although you did not know it.

50. Many have made you believe that you are outside the House of God and that therefore you have to do something to get into it. But I tell you that you are already in the House of God and you must awaken unto this Truth.

51. You are the only one who can open the door through realisation. And as the Christ unfolds in you, you will realise that you are in the Father's House and can feast from His bounteous table laden with all good things.

52. This is the glory of the Truth of the one Everlasting Almighty in Whom we live and move and have our Being, and this Truth shall set you free.

53. I am the Love and Wisdom of God, therefore listen to me in your hearts, for there I dwell.

54. Let my heart and your heart beat as one ; and then, throughout the outer, including your body of flesh, will kindle with the Light of Life, for the Lord and King has spoken, and every cell of your body will awaken to the truth of the Living Presence that is within you, and whatever you do will prosper.

55. My heart and your heart must beat as one. Do not pass over this lightly but in your heart feel deeply what it means.

56. Remember the Christ is your life and every enemy is subdued, including death. To die in Christ is to live forever.

57. If you, while in the mortal sense, could only lift your eyes and see what is around you, you would no longer disbelieve what I have told you. Your own loved ones are here with you now.

58. They are joyful in the realisation that you are receiving the Truth which many of them did not receive while on earth, thereby entering into the inner realm in ignorance of the everlasting Life.

59. What wonderful compensation you will have when you enter into the inner realm, consciously realising that there is no death, that there is no interruption in the individual life by the advent of death. Death is but a change that takes place where the Spirit sown in the earthly body goes forth in the Spiritual body. It is the

Christ that lives now in your earthly state, it is the Christ that lives forever.

60. Therefore be steadfast, strong, immovable, so that you increase day by day ; even if you do not see immediate results steady growth takes place, even in the darkness.

61. Many of you are saying to yourselves, " I am not growing at all, I do not seem to have moved forward one jot." You cannot judge yourselves as regards your growth —a flower does not know that it grows, but it does grow.

62. Some will say, " Why, I have grown ever so much more than others." Let me tell you this ; self-aggrandisement is of no value, for little children make up the Kingdom of Heaven.

63. The flowers bloom and their scent fills the air, and everyone gazes at their beauty, yet they are unaware of it. That is the state which you must cultivate also.

64. For the seeds you plant in Heaven will grow apace —your Father tendeth them.

65. Like the mustard seed which is the smallest of all seeds, yet when sown in fertile ground becomes a tree so large that wild birds can come and roost on its branches, this is like unto the Kingdom of Heaven within. All those who need rest will come unto me. You will be able to rest in me because you know the Truth of me.

66. When this seed of the Truth is planted it grows apace, yet it grows unconsciously in the individual who is conscious only of the Divine, where the greatest and the smallest are *one*.

67. Know that the most exalted and the most humble are the expression of the one Divine Spirit. Then the humblest becomes the greatest and the greatest becomes the unassuming.

68. This is my peace, this is my love, this is the power of the Christ that dwells in every soul. So be it with you.

69. When a seed is sown in the darkness of the earth it grows because of the power within, the seed reproduces like unto itself and thereby is multiplied one hundredfold.

70. So it is with you all. The seed of the Christ is sown in the darkness of the world ; this seed is the light of the world and the darkness did not overcome it.

71. The darkness of the earth does not overcome the seed which is planted in its bosom ; neither does the darkness of the world overcome the seed of the Christ that is planted in you.

72. When you become aware of yourself one with the Christ, the only begotten Son of the Father, I tell you, this is the seed which grows, unconsciously revealing Its Divine Nature to everyone.

73. There is peace and love in the heart. So it is with all of you ; the seed of the Christ is sown in the darkness of the world and this seed is the light of the world.

74. The darkness in the world is the friendly evil like the darkness of the earth ; it hastens the growth of the light of the world which shines to light the path of all on the way to freedom.

75. The so-called evil has caused the seed to quicken, to bring forth the power and the glory of the Christ, for I have overcome the world.

76. When you look upon evil as something that is overwhelming and real, then by your own consciousness you give it a power it does not possess. Understand that this darkness is kindly and enables the seed of the Christ to grow from victory to victory.

77. This is assured, because it has already been ordained by the great Almighty. It is the Truth existing before Time began, and this same Truth is now as it will be forever the same.

78. It is for this that you are born in the world to overcome the world through the victory of the Christ of

God within you, and this victory is assured, for the Lord of Hosts has decreed it.

79. The growth of the Christ within you is assured. The Christ is perfect in himself, always has been and always will be, because he was the Light of the World from the beginning. But as it is necessary for you as individuals to grow into the complete understanding of the Immortal Self, you are born into the earth plane.

80. You become greater and greater through your experience as you expand into boundless space. Perhaps you have not yet grasped the Truth of the saying " boundless space," but if you in your mind see that there is no space anywhere, all being filled with the Mind of God, then there can be no outside It ; It fills boundless space.

81. The manifested Universe is continually expanding and will go on expanding eternally in the Infinite Universe, never ceasing. Through your experience in this plane of action, so you are able to help in this expansion.

82. You who are now living upon earth will come to the inner where I am ; you will not only see the work that is being done upon this planet, but you will also be in contact with forces, Spiritual Forces, which are working in other planets, and in the inner realm we meet and talk with each other.

83. These are all the expressions of the Almighty, not separate from Himself but in Himself, expanding through Him and creating through Him continuously world after world, Universe after Universe. This is your eternal progress into Infinity.

84. Now think of your mortal sense how small it is, how limited you have allowed yourselves to be, confined to the state of mortal sense.

85. How limited you have allowed your consciousness to be, affected by the mortal sense. When you come to the inner you will see how ignorant you have been of the

Truth ; yet I tell you, and I tell you truly, that it is the Father who is working in you now.

86. Therefore, my brothers and sisters, be steadfast, abounding in the work of overcoming the world. Your labour is not in vain, for I am with you always.

87. In Nature herself is all that is seen in the outer ; the very creative process is in the inner. There is nothing you see in the outer but that which is an expression of the inner. The inner is the real cause, the outer is the effect.

88. Be not dismayed by scenes in Nature which you think should not be, because all is working towards the all-good.

89. For all that exists is first in the real world, of which yours is but the shadow.

90. When my task is fulfilled the earth shall no longer be the outer shadow, but will be the Kingdom of the Christ, where the lion and the lamb lie down together.

91. The lion is the symbol of the carnal flesh, the lamb is the symbol of the Lamb of God, the Christ, so that the outer shall be the inner and the inner the outer. The lion shall not overcome the lamb, but the lamb shall overcome the lion.

92. The lion of the carnal flesh shall disappear, and the love of God shall dwell in freedom. It was this that was brought very strongly to my consciousness while I lived on earth, when I saw that force could never bring peace and happiness to the world, because that which force brought into existence could exist only by force.

93. But when love came into the world, Love would be established. Love requires no effort to retain Its hold. This I have come again to tell you of the Christ, the Love of God. By becoming aware of this Love within yourselves you will help to bring this Love into the world.

94. Then the new heaven and the new earth shall be as one and become the dwelling place of the Most High.

95. Then all former things shall have passed away and God and man are united consciously as " one " ; thus when you have seen Me you have seen the Father.

96. I will give them one heart, and the one Spirit will be within them. I will remove their hard nature and give them a nature that can be touched, that they may live by My laws, and so they shall be My people and I willbe their God.

97. This is the promise that is being fulfilled and will be fulfilled. What has been decreed by the Lord of Hosts, so shall it be.

98. The seed of the Christ within you contains the complete fullness of the Godhead.

99. I am with you, and my work is to complete in you the fullness of the Christ of God. Therefore there is always growth, though you may not recognise it.

100. Always growth, remember ! Do not look for it, just allow yourselves to grow in the Truth. It is the beautiful harmony of Love that brings peace to all ; and through this peace there is growth.

101. When I move among you I know perfectly well that you feel the influence of my Love. I want you also to feel the influence of the Christ within your own souls, so that this peace, this love, this power, which I have can also be yours.

102. The Spiritual is always perfect ; the carnal is often out of harmony and has many imperfections born of ignorance, reacting to ignorance generation after generation.

103. Nevertheless, through the darkness, the seed of the Light of the World is pushing forward in many hearts and minds, and for this the Father sent me into the world.

104. Think what has happened since nearly 2,000 years ago—the crude state of mind that then existed among the

people; only a very few knew the Truth, for very few could understand it.

105. Even with my own disciples, it was difficult to teach them, yet when they grasped the significance of the great Truth they became my disciples, as you are now my disciples, and with the power that was invested in them through the Christ that dwelt within them.

106. The fire of the Spirit that rested upon them, and kindled the power of the Christ of God—this same will happen to you also.

107. Just as the seed attracts that which is like unto itself, and grows apace, so does the seed of the Christ grow in you, attracting Its like to grow and express Itself in your own soul. This is the only power you can ever use.

108. And to those who know they are born of the Spirit, born in His image and likeness, I reveal the truth so that they shall know as they are known.

109. Many of you have sought help from without, some of you have followed this teacher and that teacher. This has confused you and prevented the real work that can be done only from within.

110. How difficult it is for you, is it not, when you read book after book and try to conform to this idea and that idea. You follow this dogma and that creed, this cult and that cult, you try to conform to these various beliefs, how confusing it is to the soul.

111. But when I tell you within you the Christ dwells, he alone lives, he is the only begotten son of the Father, and when you begin to see this truth and become aware of yourselves as the sons and daughters of God, born of the Spirit, for I have already told you that your Father in Heaven is your only Father ; call no man your Father on earth for one is your Father which is in heaven.

112. Many of you who have sought help must now listen to the Christ *within yourselves*.

113. You must learn that the Spirit of Christ in you is the rightful ruler in your life. Do not heed the blind that lead the blind, for you now begin to see the Truth of the only " one " Living God.

114. The Christ is the leaven in the dough. The dough is humanity and requires this leaven, so that all may become leaven through the Christ united in all.

115. And whatever you ask remembering me, even if the skies be clear, my Father will give you showers of rain for every blade of grass in the field.

116. I have spoken to you in this way, so that you can heed my words. Every blade of grass can also be every soul, and every soul is watered by the showers of God, the showers of the Spirit of Love, Wisdom and Truth. Thus every blade of grass will be washed by the rain that comes down from heaven.

117. Know ye not that it is the Father alone who does these things. In God alone all things take shape. Nothing can take shape without Him nor outside Him.

118. If you look into the skies and see the clouds gathering, you say there is going to be rain. Let me tell you, even if the skies be clear, remembering me if you ask the Father for rain He will send it, believing in me.

119. It is this power I used to walk upon the water, to feed the thousands with the few loaves and fishes at hand.

120. These were not miracles but " understanding " that I was the means through which the Father fed His flocks. " Feed my people," yet I also fed them with the Spirit of Life.

121. I gave them words of Truth that could sustain them, but they desired food, physical food, and when their bodies were satisfied with material food they said a miracle was performed. They did not understand the Truth, that this very power was within themselves.

122. How difficult it is to give Spiritual food to the masses ! Many will throw away the Spiritual food, they seek the physical rather than the Spiritual. But if you seek the Spiritual food, I tell you that all shall henceforth be given unto you. Seek ye first the Kingdom of God and use It rightly, then all things shall be added unto you.

123. Your hearts must be one heart in the body of the Lord of Hosts.

124. So much of your suffering is unnecessary, caused by struggling to rid yourselves of that which is attracted from the outer.

125. Remember that *nothing* can oppose the will of God, lie content and rest in the Lord, and the Christ shall be your warrior. He alone will set you free.

126. Every experience will render you more power ; learn that the beauty of the morning sun comes after the darkness of the night.

127. How truly wonderful it is, that those who have seen the light and understand it, even in the darkness they will have faith, for they understand.

128. After the darkness of the night the beauty of the morning sun will shine. Let my peace be with you. Let this power of the Christ work in you.

129. Sorrow brings you nearer to me, to learn of me, so that your sorrow will be turned into joy.

130. From this day forth you are my Father's children. In the night He lays you down to sleep and in the morning awakens you, for He loveth you as a mother loveth her babe.

131. The heart of the babe is empty of all things except its mother, so let your heart be empty of all things except your Father which is in Heaven, and He will possess your heart wholly.

132. The glory of this Truth opens you to the Love of God, to the Peace and Harmony and the strength and the

power of the mighty Presence, and in this peace there is power and freedom.

133. You can say to the waves "Be still" and they shall be still. But the stillness must be first in your hearts through the recognition of the Father, for He alone must fill your heart and mind.

134. You can do what pleases Him, only when you leave your heart open to Him at all times.

135. There is nothing more sweet and delightful than the continual conversation with your Heavenly Father who loves you. Only those who can comprehend this can practise and experience it.

136. Do not do it for pleasure or exercise but from the heart full of Love. How many of you practise the truth for exercise, for experience, for the pleasure it gives you, and for what you can gain by it ?

137. Remember what I say, let your heart be one in the heart of the Lord of Hosts. Think what it means. Contemplate this, and, as you begin to think of this deeply, it will go deeper and deeper until such time as you become like unto me, made in His image and likeness, for I am His Son, I do His bidding, the will of the Father is done in me. And when you have seen me you have seen the Father, I am the Love of God, the only begotten Son of the Father of Love.

Now let us enter into the Sanctuary of the Most High.

Silence

MY PEACE AND MY LOVE REMAIN WITH YOU

(The Scribe's Remarks :

During the whole of this lesson heavenly music could be dimly heard, and this added tremendous power to the Master's words.)

TALK 10

BLESSED ARE THE PURE IN HEART: FOR THEY SHALL KNOW GOD

My peace and my love I bring with me to remain with you.

1. Intellectual knowledge is not enough ; only with an understanding heart can you know the Father.

2. The mind can reason, and reason is good, but this knowing must go further than reason. You must feel it, you must know it in your heart.

3. Before you can truly feel, your heart must also be full of Love. This is the Christ, the manifesting power in the world, the power that sustains the whole of humanity.

4. Individually it works for you when you recognise it as the whole. As you become aware of the wholeness of this power within you, you feel it, you know it, you become Love Itself.

5. The heart is the doorway to Divine Wisdom, and this can be understood only in your own heart.

6. The mind leads you to reason, to know that which is false, and to know and understand that which is true. The mind is the gateway to the heart, but unless the heart is full of the Christ-Love, then the power of the Christ is not in you.

7. The mind can effectively reason, but the understanding I mean goes just further than reason—a knowing of that which is behind and beyond the mind, the cause of all creation.

8. There is only one truth, and I am repeating what I know in many ways. This is the easiest and best means I know, and I use no other.

9. There are many who pick up ideas, words, phrases, which they repeat, but to do this is of very little value. Sayings and repetitions that are without understanding are

of very little value in developing the power of the Christ Power, which is Love and Wisdom.

10. What I mean is this. When you begin to understand in your own heart, and the heart becomes pure, the Christ dwells there. Sayings and ideas belong to the mind, but it is the heart that really feels beyond ideas. Ideas are not Truth, sayings are not Truth, beliefs are not Truth. Truth is beyond all these.

11. There is a knowing that goes beyond reason, a knowing that goes beyond sayings or ideas, for ideas and sayings are but words when there is no understanding.

12. I am revealing Reality, a Living Existing Reality. You do not create Reality with an idea, nor can you understand it through ideas or by saying words ; you can only understand it when you open your heart to It and when you discern all that is not Reality.

13. It gives you freedom, freedom to express that which is true. Therefore it is for this I have come, to make you free from all that is false.

14. It is not an idea, it is not a saying, it is not a belief, it is not a product of your imagination, it is not anything that can be conjured up in the mind. It already is complete, living, expressing Itself now. It is all the Power there is. It is the ever-present Life in which there is neither past nor future, only the Eternal Now.

15. In order to know the Father of Love you must think of Him often ; then your heart will be where your treasure is.

16. Some imagine that it is a waste of time dwelling on God. But I urge you to think of the mighty power that is behind all Creation, feel It, understand It by discerning all that is relative to It.

17. As you begin to feel the warmth of Its Love and the Wisdom of Its creative power, you begin to feel that you belong to Reality ; then you give expression to Its Love and Wisdom.

18. Is it then not worth while to dwell upon God and all the wonderful ways in which He expresses Himself in and through us and in all Creation ?

19. This is very important to you, and it deserves your deep contemplation. I know the way ; that is why I say, Follow in my footsteps.

20. The true revelation must unfold from the Divine Heart of Love, beating in unison with your own, so near is the Father. It is the Father, who ever remaineth within me, revealing Himself.

21. The Divine Heart is beating in unison with your own when you feel the Divine Heart within your own, beating as one with your own heart.

22. Love draws a veil over all wrong-doing, while hate stirs up strife. Do not live in the duality of the mind, but seek the oneness of the Spirit.

23. You must draw the veil of love over wrong-doing, so that hate does not enter into the heart. This Mighty Power of Love overcomes all things. Love is of God ; good and evil are of man's mind.

24. No matter what is done to you, no matter what is said about you, you must not seek revenge, because, unless your heart is full of Love, Love cannot express Itself. Freedom comes to you only by giving your heart to Christ, so that the Christ can possess it wholly.

25. This is the only living Power, the only Living Reality ; and when you discern all that which is false, you will no longer hinder the expression of that which is true.

26. Good sense is always on the lips of the pure in heart, while the senseless talk folly.

27. The pure in heart give expression to that which is true, while the senseless, not knowing the Truth, talk folly.

28. A fool's babbling will always bring trouble, while silence and wisdom pour oil on troubled waters.

29. You come here for a purpose, to learn the deeper

understanding, so that you also may become my disciples. To know yourselves is the first thing to do ; then the power that can overcome all conditions will manifest. To know the self you must become aware of the ways of the self, and this leads to freedom. In the self is the cause of all misery.

30. You must be my example to show the world the true Christ Principle, which is love thy neighbour as thyself.

31. The words of the Christ will make many wise, while the views of the ignorant are of little worth.

32. My words to you are like rare silver, and pure as the rarest of gold. Take heed and apply them to yourselves.

33. It is the blessing of the Father that brings wealth and happiness ; never does it bring trouble with it.

34. Whatsoever you ask in my name, so the Father shall bless you with. This is the promise : Ask, knowing the Christ as the only begotten son of God, the only existing Power in you. It is the Father Himself expressing Himself in you. There is no separation : I in you, you in me, and we in the Father, all in the Father, and the Father in all.

35. The blessing of the Father is beyond our comprehension. His Love is always expressing Its mighty Power for the benefit of all.

36. For when the storm comes, the foolish are swept with the swirl, but those pure in heart are deeply rooted in Christ, the only begotten Son of the Father.

37. I am speaking these Truths to you by means of the voice, to be taken down so that you can read them and dwell upon them for further enlightenment.

38. To hear the voice stirs your soul in recognition of the Truth that I am alive, " I am the Life." As you are alive now, you will know also that I am alive with you, and as I am so shall you be also.

39. I am not separated from you, as many would like

you to believe. The way to me is through your own hearts, for I dwell within you. Seek me and you shall find me.

40. The world is dazed by the outside illusion, and many are confused. By the inherent power within they create their own confusion.

41. Man is dazed by the illusions of the senses. Yet the inner working of the Spirit within man is unfolding the Christ of God in man, and soon the illusion of the senses will pass away.

42. What is happening in the world to-day is but the stirring of the Spirit in mankind.

43. The restlessness of the Spirit is Its unfoldment, but we see many unfolding in ignorance injuring themselves and others. If all knew the Truth of the unfoldment from within, then peace would come, but I say that peace *is* here, for Love is the foundation of the world.

44. What is in the beginning is now. That which was sent forth in the beginning is existing now, yet mankind has not yet taken hold of the Tree of Life. He still eats of the fruit of the tree of good and evil, which has its roots in himself.

45. By coming into me you shall be raised out of your condition. I am enthroned within you, yet you looked without and found me not. Look within and there find God. The pure in heart shall know Him.

46. When the mind is confused, there can be no peace ; I am not confused, I know that I am the Life. If your mind is confused by various ideas and beliefs which keep you separated from one another, then you can never know the " One " Eternal God.

47. The pure in heart see God in everyone. Beliefs, ideas, images, these are but the product of the mind, but Reality is Eternal and ever-expressing Itself in the now.

48. Mankind is raised up by realising his own Divine

Mastery through Divine understanding and Love. Thus the pure in heart shall know God.

49. As I talked to my disciples about these things, so do I talk to you of the very same things ; for you are also my disciples *in* the world to-day, and I am working in your midst.

50. Knowledge is born of suffering until man attains to the consciousness of God. When you reach the conscious awareness of the only one Real and existing Power expressed in yourselves, you will realise that suffering has been the means of the unfoldment of this awareness, and then suffering ceases.

51. During the next few years a great advancement in science will be made in the world. Much of it will uplift mankind, yet much will also be used to injure man on earth.

52. Here again is the intellect being used without the guidance of the Spirit—the pure in heart.

53. The world is still eating of the fruit of the Tree of Knowledge of Good and Evil, and only when mankind takes hold of the Tree of Life—the Christ within—will his salvation come.

54. I dealt with this question before, and I know that many of you understand it. Good and evil are not realities. Reality is neither good nor evil. It is complete in Itself, perfect in Itself. The standard of one man's evil may be another man's good, and the standard of another man's good may be another man's evil. They are relative, what man thinks.

55. If you examine closely what you think about things, you will find these are external to you and are therefore relative to you. If you call it good or evil you will know that it is relative to you. Know that you are controlled and directed by a power that is within yourselves, a power which is neither good nor evil but perfect in Itself. This is the Christ of God.

56. Good and evil are the products of your mind, what you think about things. This is the Tree of Knowledge of Good and Evil, the fruit whereof you must not eat lest you die in your ignorance. When you take hold of the Tree of Life, the innermost perception of Truth, this shall be your salvation.

57. When you know the Christ your mind is no longer troubled with good or evil, and you become the manifesting power of God's Love, Wisdom and Power.

58. I am the salvation of the world and anyone who believes in me shall live forever.

59. I am the living Christ of God whom the Father sent into the world to save the world. This same Christ dwells within. The same Spirit of God that dwells in me dwells in you.

60. Many who are listening now to me have left the earth ; they are conscious living beings who were once like you and are the same as you are now except that they have a body of a finer nature. Nevertheless, they have a body that is relative to the consciousness within, just as your body is relative to you and is under your direction when the Christ Power is understood.

61. Stretch forth thine hand and take hold of this Tree of Life, for it is the Spring of Living Water rising up to Eternal Life.

62. Most people in the world have developed through ignorance and have not developed perfectly all round ; and this has been the cause of much sickness in the world.

63. Yet it is better to come to the understanding of your Spiritual self through suffering, through experience, than without it, for this is the kindly evil in the world that aids your understanding, and develops the Christ power by observing all that is false.

64. There is nothing to fear, no matter what ails you, no matter in what circumstances you may be—the Christ

overcomes all. This is your power, the power of God existing in you. It is the creative power that exists in you from the beginning and shall be forever the same in and out of the body. Thus all power has been given unto you in heaven and on earth.

65. You are not bound by your body but you are bound in your mind by believing in the power of evil. Take hold of the Tree of Life ; this shall set you free.

66. Through the Tree of Life the undeveloped man will awaken also, and will learn of the " I am," the only Creative Power in God and in man. " I am the Life."

67. All will awaken to the Truth, but it is better that the Truth is not fully revealed until such times as the heart becomes pure.

68. The Creative Power in man is a mighty power indeed, and, when the consciousness becomes aware of it, there must be love to guide and direct Its action.

69. The Divine Heart of Love must beat in unison with your own. It reveals Itself without struggle when you are aware of the Truth. Many people have developed, but are ignorant of the Truth, and thus have created sickness and difficulties for themselves.

70. When the Truth is known and when these things are seen as relative, the Christ stands above them all, he becomes the eliminator of all adverse circumstances and conditions.

71. You cannot comprehend the greatness of the Christ in you, for the Christ is ever unfolding the Presence of God that dwelleth in the soul of man.

72. In every existing soul in the world there dwells the presence of God, and the Christ is unfolding this Presence continuously.

73. The Christ sees and understands that which is false and that which is true. The Christ also corrects the error, and when the error is corrected the condition disappears.

The Christ is the mediator between God and mankind ; he understands God and understands man. It is the *individualisation* of the Spirit of God Himself in manifestation.

74. The Father individualised in you becomes the Christ in you. The Christ then knows God and knows man. The Christ understands the weaknesses of the flesh, understands the sufferings of the world. The Christ of humanity can never be understood until you reach the selfless Christhood in yourselves.

75. You have much to learn about this, you can only know the full meaning of the sacrifice of the Cross of humanity when you enter into the selfless Christhood.

76. "I am " the Universal man and in me all will find their true relationship.

77. We are all born of the one Father, and, as you grow into this understanding, so you reach the completeness of the Christhood in yourselves. Thus you are freed from the world of illusion.

78. My voice, this knowledge, this truth, is being heard not only by you but also by many who are at present invisible to you, for there is no separation. The only separation is in man's mind, for in Reality there is no separation.

79. I am the vine, the Father is the sap in the vine, and all humanity is the branches.

80. The one tree with many branches, yet only the one Life in all. Thus I drew the simile, as you draw also the simile with reference to what you call electricity.

81. Electricity is a degree of Life in manifestation, but electricity is everywhere—there is nowhere it is not. So you draw upon it and you use it as power and light and in many other ways.

82. We are well aware of the many inventions that are taking place in the world to-day. Your scientific minds are

channels through which the Intelligence is being expressed. For all must be known to mankind on earth. You will understand and see behind the scenes, gradually becoming aware of your Divine Nature that is perfect in Itself.

83. When that recognition comes then I, the Universal man, and through the Universal man all races, shall understand one another, for that relationship will be brother.

84. I am truly the Son of God while being the son of man, so the great unity of God and man is revealed in the Cross. Death never touched the Son of God, for He is the Christ and has victory over death.

85. For the Christ dies in the flesh, only to live in the Spirit, and I am He who liveth with the Father forever and those who believe in Me will do likewise.

86. Do not think that you have to die to live with the Father, because you are living with the Father now, and in the Father, and the Father is living in you. If you can comprehend these words, then you will see that there is no separation, and no death.

87. The Father is Infinite in nature and to be Infinite He must include all, otherwise He could not be infinite. He must exist in you, also, and you must exist in Him, otherwise you could not live—because there is no outside of the Father ; He is complete in Himself.

88. You are created by Him and in Him, and in Him you live, and the life in you is eternal because It is His Life. I and the Father are one.

89. There is no power that can harm you against your own will.

90. It was for this I entered into the astral groves where souls lived in the darkness of their own ignorance :

91. To set them free and to cast off that which separates them from God, so that all may live in the reality of the Christ.

92. Many who are now hearing my voice, at this time are being liberated from the astral groves, to enter into Paradise, for it was their own ignorance only that enveloped them in the darkness of their own making.

93. Many have found that their beliefs are only beliefs, and have no existence in Reality, for Reality is Eternal. It is the only existing Creative Living Principle. When the Eternal Reality is realised, then you are free.

94. I spoke of the time that I entered into the astral groves. Little did you realise the conditions I had to take on myself to enter into those groves to free those in darkness. You can understand only when you realise that I suffer with the whole of humanity, for I am Humanity, and thus I have come to free humanity.

95. There are many who are now working in these groves liberating those in darkness. For all must become " One " and perfect according to the fullness of the Christ.

96. THEREFORE HENCEFORTH BE NOT DECEIVED BY FALSE DOCTRINES THAT SEPARATE YOU EVEN IN CHRIST, FOR THOSE WHO PREACH CHRIST AND SEPARATION AT THE SAME TIME, ARE FALSE TEACHERS.

97. As the body is guided by " One," even all joints although separated, they are guided through the One that has full care of the body.

98. Therefore know ye not that I live not only for one nation but for all nations, for all are the children of my Father which is in Heaven.

99. Then let all bitterness and anger against your brother be put away from you.

100. Seek not revenge, for that which is in your own heart will befall you also.

101. What a man thinketh in his heart so is he.

102. Many of those who have passed from the physical

body are watching, helping and guiding others in the physical. Each and every one of you has an angel guide ; you are never left alone for a moment.

103. When you enter into the world as a babe, yes, before you enter the world as a babe, there is an angel guide with you, one who continues with you even after you leave the physical body until you reach maturity of Spiritual sense.

104. You may also one day be one of those angel guides to someone you love. It is not always one nearest and dearest to you on earth who becomes your guide. It is often one who you have never known while on earth but one who is united to you in the Spiritual.

105. Seek not revenge, for that which is in your own heart will befall you also. If you can understand these words, then you see the meaning of the double-edged sword. Whatever you think in your own heart about anyone else you create in yourselves.

106. Be kind to one another and tender-hearted, forgiving one another. As God forgives you, so must you forgive one another for my sake.

107. To be pure in heart is to be God-like as beloved children of my Father.

108. For there is but one God and one Christ in God, and one God in Christ ; and this Christ dwells in you and is your only Reality—your Real Self. Then be yourself, be ye perfect as your Father in Heaven is perfect.

109. Can you understand the true meaning of these words ? Be yourself, be ye perfect as your Father in Heaven is perfect.

110. Man's ignorance of this great truth is his inward poverty which makes him look outside himself for things to cherish, yet his poverty still remains.

111. This is the hell man makes for himself, for he finds no comfort in the things of the world which he cherishes ;

even if he clings to them he will lose them, for he cannot take them with him.

112. I am the everlasting happiness, the wealth and strength that lives forever ; and through the water that I give you to drink, you will never thirst any more, for it is the Eternal Spring of Life that gives all things to those who ask, knowing me.

113. And how would you know me ? You know me through understanding the source of your being, for the power of creation is within you.

114. Keep perfect poise within, never allowing any outside influence to enter into the innermost to disturb you.

115. In helping others, it is far better to show them how to help themselves through the Creative Power of the Christ that dwells within them.

116. To help others of yourself is not the plan. Little has been done even if you clothe and feed the needy while leaving out the real gift of the Christ Spirit, the victor in all circumstances, the victor who dwells within every soul.

117. The great truth that you must hand to every soul is the power of the Christ that dwells within them. This is the great gift of God.

118. Let everyone see the Christ in you through understanding, for victory dwells within oneself. To give is divine, but to give understanding of the Christ power is the secret behind all true happiness; It is the wisdom of God.

119. I have come to open the door that separates you and me.

120. This is the door of the outer senses and because you lived in the outer you did not know the inner.

121. Yet the outer is but a reflection of the inner. Remember the desires of the flesh are also supplied from

within. But there is an end to all things of the flesh, while the things of the Spirit are eternal.

122. I do not ask you to reject the things of the flesh, they are necessary while in the body, yet the things of the Spirit are more important.

123. Nor must you despise the things of the flesh, but realise and recognise their value and use them accordingly.

124. They are not realities in themselves ; they are only a means to an end, not the end itself. Then I say to you that the desires of the flesh and the things of the flesh shall come to an end, while the things of the Spirit shall remain.

125. The personality is the illusion of the senses, yet true personality is the translation of the Divine Spirit into daily action.

126. Only by withdrawing myself from the midst of my disciples could I come to them free from the illusion of the personality of Jesus.

127. It was this interior sense that made my disciples the great Apostles that they were, because and only by this same interior sense can I make you also realise the great importance of the truth I am revealing to you.

128. You must not think of the personality of Jesus the man, nor must you image this personality, because this will blind you to the Truth of the Christ. The Christ is the only begotten Son of the Father, the power that is behind all manifestation.

129. The word was in the beginning, and that word was with God, that very word that was God, and that word that was made flesh. Personalities must fade out of your minds before you can see the reality of the Christ. This is the meaning of my words, " What is it you have come out to see, a man ! "

130. Only by entering into the Universal Christ can you become true individuals of the Christ Spirit revealing the truth of the " one " God.

131. I in you and you in me and we in them and all in the Father.

132. And here we are assembled together all filled with the Holy Spirit of God our Father ; therefore we will echo that word that was with God and is God, LOVE.

133. Let us now realise the feeling of our Father's Love for all.

MY PEACE AND MY LOVE I LEAVE WITH YOU TO REMAIN WITH YOU

Let us enter into this true state of Love where the Divine Heart beats in all hearts.

Do not close your eyes but look towards me.

SILENCE

MY PEACE, MY LOVE I LEAVE WITH YOU

(THE SCRIBE'S REMARKS :

During this Silence a great light enveloped the brother ; nothing was seen but a blinding light. Then the Master took his departure and the brother remained standing. Truly a wonderful demonstration of the power of the Spirit.)

TALK 11

THE SPIRIT OF GOD IS PERSONIFIED IN THE CHRIST OF GOD IN YOU

My peace, my love I bring to you.

1. It is the Christ that is the personal expression of the Almighty. This Christ dwells in you and in every living soul. This is your life, your consciousness. By It you live, by It you are made eternal, through It you have salvation.

2. This is the great Cosmic Consciousness, the inner illumination which will cover the whole earth. When this is understood by each and every one so the whole earth will be transformed, transformed out of its state of ignorance through the realisation of the Truth.

3. As the Universal in each individual is recognised, so will It become universal. Thus the Whole which is behind the individual will be realised by each individual.

4. The Universal, individualised, is the Christ, and this must be recognised by the individual. Then the individual will know that the whole is behind him and behind the whole of humanity, for there is no division. The full realisation of this reveals God in man.

5. In God there is no division. There is but one Whole expressing Itself in the many, and God's Consciousness is manifesting in every one of His creations, and every one of His creations exists in His Consciousness. God in the midst of thee is mighty.

6. When you begin to understand this, then you will raise your consciousness out of the conditions that surround you and enter into your true birthright, the Christ of God within.

7. The world will then emerge from the limitation of time and space and gain its Spiritual freedom.

8. Time and space have always been the hindrance to the understanding of wholeness, the completeness of the Infinite. To recognise Infinity there cannot be time or space.

9. Reality had no beginning and will have no ending. Reality is not created by man but man creates time and space, in his own consciousness. This is the illusion, the not understanding and realising wholeness. This is the illusion, not understanding and realising wholeness where there is no time, no space, no beginning, no ending. There is but one whole, and this whole is expressing Itself now. This is Reality. I am one with Reality ; Reality and I are one. This is the recognition of the Christ Consciousness wherein all is possible.

10. Look beyond the personality, it is but the outer manifestation. You cannot find Truth outside yourselves. You must look beyond the personal self and the personalities around you. You can never find Truth in personality ; personality is the result of the individual's reactions to conditions.

11. Ideas and concepts held in the consciousness are being expressed through the personality, but this is not Reality. Reality is complete and perfect in Itself, and It expresses Itself in purity in perfection ; this is the Christ of God. Then look beyond the personality.

12. I know how you love the brother whom I am using as a means to transmit my thoughts to you, and some of you think he is affected when the power becomes too great for his body to stand. But I tell you truly we love him as much as you do and will see to it that no harm comes nigh him ; so be at peace and know that all is well.

13. Some of you find also that the power becomes too great for you, too strong for your bodies, and you feel as if

you are leaving your bodies. Now the way to prevent this is not to struggle for the body, and then the feeling will disappear ; and you will be perfectly conscious of my presence.

14. I am giving you this advice now, because I know how difficult it is for some of you to hold yourselves in the body when the power becomes too strong. My Spiritual power can do you no harm.

15. At the present time you are surrounded by a tremendous force of Spiritual Beings ; who are amongst you and come from all planes of consciousness. These beings are just like yourselves, the only difference being that they manifest in a higher vibration. They bring a tremendous force with them ; they come here to listen, and their love surrounds you also.

16. I know the difficulties some of you have when the emotions are strong ; these vibrations create a vibration in your emotional body, and through the emotional body they affect the physical body and consequently you feel the effect, but nothing can harm you here or anywhere else, for I am with you always.

17. The Spirit of God is personified as the Christ of God in you. Then to realise yourself one with Christ is the way to Truth. To realise yourselves with Christ, not only you in the physical plane, but also you who have passed beyond the physical plane, it is also for you too to recognise and realise yourselves one with Christ.

18. In that recognition, then, you find the salvation and the power and the glory of the Infinite Spirit which is individualised as the Christ of God in you.

19. What you gaze upon with your inner vision you bring forth into your individual life.

20. There is no secret in this. It has been told by all the prophets, yet few could realise it, because they looked outside themselves for the answer.

21. Many are doing the same to-day. The masses are looking outside for the answer. But you are learning not to look outside yourselves for the answer ; only within yourselves can you find the answer—I am the Life !

22. Become one with all, a great brotherhood divinely united one to another in God—this is the way I lead you.

23. Although this is a Reality, now it must be established in the individual consciousness to make it a Reality to the individual.

24. What you are conscious of now in your life is being expressed in your outer. That is why the unfoldment of the Spirit creates an expansion of the consciousness ; and as your consciousness envelops all, through development it grasps the greater understanding of the Truth of the Whole. As the consciousness of God holds you, so must you hold the Consciousness of God that is within you, for you are one.

25. Idols are mere gold and silver made by hands of man.

26. With mouths, but they never speak ; with eyes, but they cannot see.

27. With ears, but they cannot hear ; and no breath of life in them.

28. The ignorant worship the things that do not live, while the wise live in God.

29. Even if an idol is held as a symbol, the consciousness must be aware of that which is behind the symbol. To ignorantly worship an idol is useless, but to live in the Father and to know that He lives in you is true worship.

30. Therefore we know what we do worship, while the masses do not know what they worship. Therefore I say to you worship God in Spirit and in Reality, for God is Spirit, and the only living Being there is. I and the Father are one.

31. But I tell you, worship no one on earth, for one is your Father which is in Heaven.

32. He is the Living Breath in you, the Christ of God, individualised in you.

33. The Christ is the Love of God in all mankind. I am the Love of God, to know this Love you must adore Him who is Love.

34. And how do you adore that which is Love ? By reaching up to the highest that is within yourselves, by giving out the love that is flowing to you from Him who created you, becoming aware of this overflowing river of Life and Love that streams through your soul.

35. When you give expression to that stream of Life and Love that enters into your own soul and heart, then you will truly feel the love of God, for to love all is to love God. God loves all, for all is His Creation ; that is why I say, love your neighbour as yourself.

36. I am joyful in those who carry the tidings of peace and goodwill towards all men.

37. I am silently working in the hearts of all who listen unto me. Turn ye from without, and learn of the only " One " who dwells within.

38. In your quietness there I am dwelling in your consciousness, in your heart urging you to listen to me. The rhythm of love, of peace, of harmony in your soul is the rhythm of the Eternal Love of God animating the whole of humanity.

39. I am one with the Father, and I am not divided in any of you, but one with Him in Whom you live and have your being ; therefore in Him I am whole, in you and in all I am the same. With my peace, my love, I bless all.

40. I will open the doors so that the great River of Infinite Life will flow out and flood all nations.

41. For the vision of Daniel is being enacted in your midst.

42. It is not my purpose to reveal the vision of Daniel in these talks to you, but when you read Daniel you will

know what I mean. It is the vision of the things to come, the vision and purpose of the great Architect of the Universe, who created all planets and suns in the Universe and everything that exists therein and thereon.

43. Each planet is controlled and directed by a Spirit. Just as the Christ controls this world, so does the great Ether Spirit control the various ether planets in this Universe. These Spirits are known to us; we understand them; we commune with them, because there is no space, no time, no distance.

44. Each planet has its various degrees of influence upon the earth, all ordained by the great Architect of the Universe.

45. Daniel's vision is an understanding of the wave-lengths of the expression of these Solar Angels, Solar Angels working for the unfoldment and upliftment of this earth and all that dwells thereon. The end shall be Peace and Love. This message I bring to you, Truly I tell you that God has ordained that the end shall be Peace, Love and Goodwill between all souls.

46. There is perpetual healing wherever this River flows. Then open yourselves up to It, so that It flows through you to all creatures, and there shall also be abundance.

47. For wherever this Stream flows, so does it make alive all creatures, and there shall also be abundance.

48. This Water flows from the Sanctuary of God and is food and drink for *all* souls.

49. Little are you aware of the magnificent work that you are doing in the Sanctuary. Some of you may think that you have just come here by chance, but there is no such thing as chance in regard to these things. I have told you before that you did not choose me : it is I who choose you.

50. He who is weak in understanding faith, assist him by being consistent in your own reasoning.

51. What I mean by understanding faith is, there is a faith without understanding, that is like the house that is built upon sand, the winds and the rains come and beat upon it and it is swept away.

52. True Faith is based upon the rock of understanding ; this understanding faith is the Truth. It is like the house that is built upon the rock ; the winds and the rains come and beat upon it and it stands against all that assails it.

53. This is the understanding faith that I want you to have and to give to those who come to you to drink. Give him to drink that which shall make him *never* to thirst any more, give him the Spring of Living Water rising up to Eternal Life.

54. Do not lose yourselves in the external or be caught up with sayings. Keep your mind on the Eternal ; this is the sure way to reason.

55. Many will beset you with words ; many will come to you with sayings, perhaps some of which I have already said, yet not understanding the meaning of the words they will put a different construction upon them. But if you hold your mind on the Eternal, then that is the sure way to understand me.

56. Do not try to remember my sayings or repeat them parrot-fashion—that is of little value to you, or to any who comes to you. The word will be given unto you at that very hour. This is the well that never runs dry, and when you drink of it you shall never thirst any more.

57. Every individual who realises the Christ has won a victory for the whole race.

58. I advise you to pray often and love much and thank the Father for your glorious opportunity here and now.

59. Place yourselves in His hands, so that He may do what He pleases with you.

60. As a baby lies in the arms of its mother, feel also

that you are in the arms of the ever-Eternal Loving Father, and allow Him to do what He pleases with you. Then there shall be no struggle, and the power of God will be in your mind and heart ; your hand will be strong, your mind will be alert. This is the power of the Christ that is with you always.

61. Then He will embrace you with His Love and you will eat at His table, and serving you with His own hands He will give you the key to His treasure.

62. He will converse and delight Himself with you incessantly in thousands of ways, and He will treat you as His favourite.

63. In this way you will consider yourselves at all times in His Holy Presence ; of this I know so well.

64. It is the living power of God that dwells in you, and you can have this living power now. Recognise It and adore It, and dwell in the Holy Presence of the Father, recognising His greatness, His Love, His Power, because all is His and what is His is yours also.

65. Even the most wretched of men, full of corruption, men who may have committed all sorts of crimes against Him, have only to abandon themselves to His mercy confessing all their wickedness and asking Divine forgiveness.

66. My Father will spread before them His bounties and give them a seat at His table without rebuke.

67. For all who come to the Father through the Living Christ of God and recognise Him, He will in no wise cast out.

68. Think then of the blessings that have been bestowed upon *you*. Immediately you recognise and realise the living Christ in you, you have immediately come into the Presence of the Father. You will immediately begin to express the Love of God, and at that very moment you will be made as white as the driven snow.

69. This is the peace I bring you. The mind is no longer caught up in the net of fear of hell, neither is your mind caught up in the fear of evil, because the Christ is the victor, who has been given dominion over all things. All power has been given unto me in heaven and on earth.

70. In silent communion in the Sanctuary, rest in the knowledge that His love and healing are pouring through you, and that this River of Infinite Life is covering the whole earth.

71. The covenant was carried by the tribes of Israel as the inner Sanctuary, a symbol of the inner soul, the dwelling place of the Most High.

72. It was into this Sanctuary that the Israelites entered to speak with God. Yet the real Sanctuary is within yourselves, within your own heart ; there you can speak with God. In your heart comes the healing and the Love of God.

73. What you are doing now is going on all over the world. You will not really understand until you have left the physical, and then you will see what you have done for your brothers and sisters while on earth. You will hear these words, " Well done, my good and faithful servant."

74. Each time you realise this you will find a change growing within yourself, an ever-increasing sense of responsibility towards your fellows, expressing health, happiness and an abundant life.

75. Your body is the garment of the Spirit, the Temple of the Living God, and you are learning that Spirit is the Ruler.

76. Do not be afraid of any condition that may assail you from without. No condition or circumstance, no matter what it may be, can affect the Christ in you. The Christ is adamant, is all-power there is, being the Son of God.

77. The Christ is not affected by conditions external to

the self ; the Christ is the Spirit of God in you. The Spirit is all-power and can overcome all conditions. Through suffering you gain experience, and learn of the Christ, and even if you die in suffering the Christ in you shall live joyously and will be your Eternal Reality.

78. The darkness that surrounds you is the kindly evil that unfolds the Christ in you. As the seed is planted in the kindly darkness of the earth, the Life in the seed unites with the Life in the earth waiting to reproduce it ; it grows out of the darkness to express itself in the image and likeness of the seed sown. So does the Spirit of God ; the Christ is the seed that is in you, and shall grow out of the darkness that surrounds you. The beauty of the Christ shall manifest in you as the image and likeness of the Father. I am he who liveth, who died, and now liveth forever.

79. Do not be discouraged if immediate results are not forthcoming. Work is being done in accordance with your thought. This law is infallible.

80. The darkness that seems to cover your consciousness will prove friendly, for the Christ is working in you, and failure is impossible.

81. The body of humanity will become the beautiful garment of the Spirit of God, I shall come again to tell you that salvation is not in part but with the whole, and for this I am working in your midst.

82. The signs are in the sky heralding the new Jerusalem.

83. All movements in the heavens are thoughts expressed by the Absolute. You are His thought also, and you must therefore manifest His Love and Healing.

84. Perhaps you have misunderstood the true meaning of thought.

85. Thought is not a mental concept or an image, though these find their avenue through the mind.

86. Thought is the direct expression of the thinker and is never separate from the thinker. It is the creative process behind all form and expression.

87. When you have a concept in your mind you are dwelling upon the concept ; you are looking upon something external to yourselves. Reality is behind the thought ; real thinking is when thought is not influenced by the external. This is the true expression of the thinker. My healing thought goes out to you and accomplishes its mission.

88. All worlds with their countless forms in Nature are thoughts expressed by the Infinite, in the Infinite.

89. Love is the power behind all His creations, no matter how you may view them from without. His nature invested in them is moving towards the central reservoir of Love, where all exists.

90. When you understand the whole of Nature you will see the manifestation of the Spirit of God—the manifestation of the Spirit in the mineral, the vegetable, the animal and the human. The Christ Consciousness is the recognition of the wholeness of Spirit, the Consciousness of God in man, aware of Itself. I am the Son of God, no man is my father on earth, one only is my Father who is in heaven.

91. As all rivulets move towards the sea, so do all forms move towards the unknowable sea of Love out of which all originate.

92. The Universal and the individual are one. In the individual, realising this, lies the well-spring of growth in which the Infinite Life in the individual evolves the individual. And immediately you become aware of this, your own Spiritual evolution begins.

93. The Christ is the completed man in God and God in man. He is the finished product. All the mighty power of God is expressed through him, all power has been invested

in Him in Heaven and on earth. He is complete in himself, he is the Son of the Father carrying with him all His attributes. So the Life in the Father has been invested in the Son, and the Son gives expression to that Life.

94. He is the only one—the Father within His own creation. Although self-existent yet never separated from His creation, indivisible in nature, yet whole and substantial in the many.

95. In looking at things through your senses, things that you can touch and feel, you say they are real but they are only the shadow of reality. Reality is that which is within, the invisible ; the substantial is the inner, the outer is the shadow.

96. So much trouble has come upon the earth because of the ignorance of the Truth. When the Truth is realised by all, then all shall look up the Spirit, because Spirit is Reality, while the outer is but the manifestation of the inner, for without the inner the outer does not exist.

97. In realising the meaning of the words " I am the Life," first of all you must know that God is Life and Life is God. Then in the expression of " I am the Life " you know what you are saying ; you undertand the meaning of the saying " I am the Life."

98. I am the Life. These words are true, and when understood have tremendous power in their expression.

99. I am the Life centred in God sending out rays of Love, Healing and Intelligence through all.

100. This Intelligence is active ; it is never static, It is always active expressing the Will of the Father. If the consciousness is unaware of this, it is lost in the things of the external, and this becomes the illusion in the mind that does not understand.

101. Then the Consciousness will express these illusions to the sorrow of the individual, but if, knowing the Spirit and understanding the power of the Spirit, the Will of the

Father shall be manifested, this is the Christ, the manifestation of the Love and Wisdom and Power of God bringing all into the one fold, and there shall be one shepherd.

102. Those of you who commune with me will feel my presence, for I am not apart from you. I and the Father are one with you.

103. Yes, and when you do call upon me, I will not fail you. All that is good for you will come to you through me.

104. The great enemy is the sense of separation, making separation a reality in the mind of man.

105. Through centuries of ignorance men and women have dared to think of themselves as complete and separate identities, looking on the suffering of humanity as something outside themselves.

106. There is no separation. What affects one must affect the whole. That is the way of the Christ of God. He is the salvation of the race.

107. Yes, I feel the suffering with the whole of humanity, yet I will lift this suffering from you, if you will but listen unto me. My way is the way of salvation. My way is the brotherhood of man and the Fatherhood of God. My way is Life, not death.

108. Are you looking on God from afar off ? If so, then you live in the separation of the senses, looking outside yourselves for Reality. Are you looking for God afar off ? Answer this question to yourselves. Think about it !

109. I have come to reveal that I am not separate from you, but one with you. This is your salvation.

110. The law of God is working out even to the smallest detail through your *earthly* Life.

111. The Earth holds within it the great interior, invisible Spiritual Forces creative and reconstructive, expressing Itself in form.

112. This great Spiritual Force is individualised in you as the Christ in you, expressing the Infinite Life in all its glory and power, with Love the central factor, for the dominion of Power is in Love, for God is Love and Love is God.

113. As I taught my disciples of the mysteries in secret, so I do the same to you.

114. Those who believe in me are my disciples now. Those who fail to do so, lose the great reward resulting from the recognition of the Christ, the only begotten Son of the Father.

115. All creation is the thought of the One, the Father breathing through mineral, vegetable, animal, human. The consciousness when aware of itself realises that It Is. And whatever the consciousness is aware of, so does it manifest. This is an immutable law of Life.

116. The Consciousness must become aware of Itself as the expression of the Consciousness of God. As the Father has life in Himself, so He granted the Son to have the same Life in himself.

117. The Father is Conscious of the Universe and all that is in it. His Consciousness is the Creative Principle in the Universe, so is His Consciousness established in the Son of man. The Father knoweth the Son, and the Son knoweth the Father. The Christ is the Son of God, and you are my brothers and sisters.

118. Life alone has Consciousness. " I am the Life."

119. Do not in your mind give Life form and then say that form is the reality. Life creates form, yet It is independent of form.

120. Do not by a mental process limit this Life through the reasoning of the mind, thus closing the avenue to the whole that is beyond your mind.

121. Do not confine Life to the forms which you see before you. Life is invisible, yet substantial, and is

omnipresent. The form is the expression of Life, the forms you see before you are but the expression of the whole of invisible Life, because the whole is never divided.

122. One day you will learn more about these things. You will see the invisible as a visible world ; yes, forms of life greater than you at present realise ; yes, even the angels of God, invisible to you at present, will be visible. Yet beyond this is the Life Eternal.

123. Life is beyond form, so do not limit Life by the form you see, form being the expression of Life. Do not limit Life through the reasoning of the mind, thereby closing out the whole that is beyond your mind.

124. Truth is not a part of Truth. The whole Truth is not seen or heard. Your unfoldment will still continue in the higher states.

125. There is but one Truth. I am the Truth, yet no one can conceive the all of Truth. I am in the whole of humanity. Within Me you are one in all, and all in one. This is ever-expanding into the whole of Truth, the Father of Love. The Spirit of God is personified as the Christ of God in you.

MY PEACE, MY LOVE I LEAVE WITH YOU

Let us enter into the Sanctuary.
Do not close your eyes but look towards me.

SILENCE

MY PEACE, MY LOVE I LEAVE WITH YOU

———

(THE SCRIBE'S REMARKS :

The Master took his departure, with the same familiar heavenly music and chimes, in a blaze of light that almost blinded the eyes.)

TALK 12

Thus the Christ has Risen

My peace, my love I bring to you.

1. Divine thought is the uprising of the Christ in you.

2. Very few understand the mighty power of the Christ in you. It is the Spirit of the Father manifesting individually in each and every one of you. Become conscious of the Father, conscious of the word of God, the medium between the outer and the inner ; this is the Christ in you.

3. When you seek within, you will find the Father ; when you look without, you see effects. You must recognise the difference between the two and become aware of the great Creative Power that is within you. This is the only Creative Power there is, and to use It consciously, recognising its source, brings about Its own perfection in your Life.

4. Then do not limit It by your own mental process of reasoning and thus close the avenue to the Unlimited. Your reason is limited to the understanding of things. Therefore you have to eliminate all limited beliefs, ideas of others, so that this unlimited state of consciousness, that is, shall enter into the individual consciousness and there flood it with a Divine Power that is beyond reason.

5. This Divine Nature Itself is capable of knowing at once without reasoning, without recollection. It is free and natural. It has within Itself the power to create, because it has unlimited understanding. It is beyond reason, because It Itself is full of Wisdom, but reason limits It when you reason about It, because It is beyond

reason ; your reason is based upon what is in the mind, but Reality is beyond your mind.

6. You cannot reason on that which is beyond your reason, but you can expand your capacity to receive by clearing your mind of limitations.

7. Your beliefs have become your hindrance to the unfoldment of the unlimited. If you were without beliefs that hinder you, you would again be as a little child, free to understand Reality, without hindrance.

8. Many are hindered because of their rigid beliefs, they cannot accept anything beyond the idea that has been given to them by others. So they give themselves over to an authority outside themselves, with the result that they are limited, bound, and are no longer free.

9. It is these hindrances, these beliefs, that prevent the tremendous power of the Christ manifesting now in you. The Christ has been given all power in heaven and on earth. When you understand this, limited beliefs disappear, because the Christ is unlimited in nature. The Christ Power is the Father Himself individualised, expressing Himself individually in each and every one of you—not separated in Himself but with variety beyond calculation ; nevertheless one and the same, because the Christ is the same in all.

10. Unless ye become as a little child you cannot enter the Kingdom. Only with the mind free from the limitation of ideas and beliefs of others can you receive the unlimited, for it is I who is working in you.

11. When your consciousness becomes aware of my unlimited nature, and this unlimited nature is found within yourselves, then you can say as I do from within, I and the Father are one. Recognising the source of Being, knowing that the same source is within all, entering into these inner realms of the Father's Nature, therefore I work in you and through you.

12. My very thoughts, my words, now are claiming your attention deep in your soul ; these words become part of yourselves and eventually they shall express themselves in your life bringing peace, harmony and joy.

13. There is so much of the Christ force imprisoned within your minds, unable to express itself because of your rigid beliefs.

14. You have only to look into a mind rigid in its belief to see how bound it is. This is truly the ignorance that hinders the manifestation of the Christ in the world, and is the cause of separation and conflict.

15. How true this is ! Even in infancy the mind is crammed with limited beliefs, and from then onwards the child grows into maturity with beliefs smothering the Christ, and not until such time as the soul awakens to the recognition of the power that is within itself can it be free. Then it casts off these limited beliefs and ideas of others, no longer bound by them, but free to express the Word that was in the beginning.

16. It was for this that I came into the world, to release all from the bonds of limitation. Look to the Father only, and through Him alone can you be free. He alone, within yourselves, is the only authority ; there is no other.

17. The flowers open and bloom by the hidden force within them ; so is the soul of man opened by the Christ Life within. Then do not hinder it by your limited mental processes.

18. How easy it is to see, yet how difficult it is for those blinded and controlled by beliefs to throw off their bondage ! They struggle for freedom, yet their ideas and beliefs bind them.

19. When all these beliefs of limitation are eliminated from the minds of men and women throughout the whole world, the world will then truly express the Christ Life.

20. All of you who have passed beyond the earth, who

have experienced Life upon the earth, know how difficult it was to throw off your rigid beliefs. Some of you still hold to them, you are still struggling for freedom. But as you gradually unfold you will find that there was no such thing as belief, there was only " knowing," the knowing of God in Whom there is no separation.

21. And when the mind of man comes to that point where it has discerned everything, and has reached the highest within itself, then it pierces the veil that has separated it from the All and enters into the completeness of the understanding of the Christ. And I ask you : " What is it that thou knowest now ? " and you reply, " I know only Christ, who is all in all."

22. When the mind of man becomes the instrument through which the Christ Power can manifest, it is truly intelligent. There is an intelligent understanding of all things, thereby creating all things anew. It is through this power that everything is created anew.

23. This is the power that is planted within yourselves and comes forth when the mind is free from all limited beliefs and ideas. True Intelligence begins to act when the mind knows no separation. *And when this is known, there is freedom from the prison of your own making.*

24. This is the result of passing through the veil that separates you from " the All-Knowing."

25. I assure you that there is no difficulty in piercing the veil ; it is simple, when you eliminate from your mind all limitations, all beliefs, all theories. When this is accomplished you can look towards me and I shall speak through you.

26. Looking at humanity from the inner, we see how much power is imprisoned by your beliefs and by the mental concepts you hold.

27. One of your great hindrances is the delusion that times of prayer ought to be different from other times.

28. Prayer is the sense of the Presence of God and this should be a conscious reality at all times.

29. You reserve one day of the week for prayer ! And because you reserve one day of the week for prayer you feel satisfied in your weekly meditations.

30. Let me tell you that that is not the way. The way must be the continual conscious awareness of the Father working in you ; you realise that there is no separation and that time and space do not exist.

31. Then do your common business, not merely to please man, but, as far as you are capable of, purely for the Love of God.

32. Thus your work will not be in any way limited, but will expand into the unlimited nature of the Presence that guides it.

33. You give yourselves over to me entirely in the recognition of the Truth that the Father can manifest Himself in all His glory and Power ; then the mind becomes a vehicle for the expression of this mighty power. But before this can be, the mind must be full of reverence, full of love. Then you will raise yourselves above your ordinary everyday life into one of glory in the " Presence " that knows not past or future. Then this mighty power becomes a reality to you.

34. Planets move in their orbits and all movements in the skies are His wonders, yet how little do you know that that same power is waiting to express itself through the mind that is capable of giving itself over entirely to the expression of the Divine Love and Power, the Christ in all.

35. You need not worry about the outcome of your labour, for your heavenly Father rewards generously all those who love Him.

36. Neither need you worry for to-morrow, for to-morrow is already taken care of by the love expressed to-day.

37. The high-lights of your lives are registered and remain with you and are carried through into the inner realm. All that is good and worthy is held ; all that is not, dissolves away. For the Father holds nothing against you—only your brother in ignorance does that.

38. All that is Christ-like is held, but all that has no power of its own must dissolve away, because it is only sustained by the illusion of the senses.

39. Fear not the things that beset you, nor the so-called evil that surrounds you, for it cannot enter the heaven within you ; these things dissolve away into nothingness, where they belong.

40. Within, you will feel that calm steadfast effect of the power of the Christ of God, the channel for the unlimited expression of the Father Himself.

41. This is the true Light which lighteth every man who cometh into the world.

42. In everyone that is born, there the Christ is born. This same Christ, this same living Spirit, is the Father expressing Himself in each and every one of His creations.

43. The world is under His hand, yet the world knows little of Him yet.

44. But to those who receive Him, so will He give to them power to overcome, as Christ the Son of God overcomes all things.

45. This is the Divine promise when you know His name and recognise Him, and become aware of the source of your being, not limited in any way. This is true freedom.

46. True freedom is knowing and understanding the source of your own Being. Great is the joy of those who have come to the Fountain and have drunk thereof. For they drink of the wine of Life, the wine that is better than all other wines ; It is the source of all Life. I am that Life, I and the Father are one.

47. Just as those who accept the Christ, the Spirit of the Father, so shall the word of God dwell in the flesh to give witness to the Truth of the only living God who governs Heaven and Earth with love.

48. Christ in you is the word of God that dwells in the flesh to give witness to the Truth of the only living God who governs heaven and earth with love. Need I explain this further to you? I will leave it with you, so that you can think it out for yourselves and thereby bring peace into your souls.

49. And unless ye shall love one another, ye shall not enter into the Kingdom of my Father.

50. For my Father's Kingdom is a Kingdom of Love, of Harmony, and when you enter into my heaven you must bring my heaven with you. This is not so difficult. First you must cast off all limitations, all ideas that lead to separation, all jealousies, all antagonisms, all that hinders the true expression of the Father Himself.

51. If you would look into your mind and see the thoughts, images and ideas, the conflicts, the sorrows, the depressions you create, all these limitations manifest in your own mind, only through not understanding the Truth.

52. Allow all these limitations that burden you to drop from you at once, and then you will be in heaven. Thus you bring heaven with you when you clear your minds of all limitations.

53. For He loveth each one of you. As a hen covereth her brood with her wings, so does my Father cover you all with His love.

54. Some hate me because they did not understand me. But you understand me, you hear me and my Father who sent me. I thank Thee, Father, that Thou hast given me these Thy children of love, that I may teach them of Thee, so that they may be free and complete as I am.

55. You cannot have enmity against another in my Father's House ; His feast is spread before all those who love each other, for in each one I dwell. If ye hate your brother you will hate me also.

56. There must be great peace in your mind, your body and environment, as God worketh in you to unfold the holy seed, for His work of creation is through you.

57. You are the place of action that God created for my manifestation.

58. Therefore you shall not weary in doing things for the Love of God, and in every thing you do, do it for the Love of God.

59. I am giving to you the secret of all power in heaven and on earth, and if you will take hold of what has been given to you and accept it now and act upon it, truly I tell you, that you will see the effects of it instantly in your lives.

60. You will not have to wait until to-morrow or a year hence, but now instantly you shall feel the effects in your lives—now ! Therefore do everything for the love of God.

61. Many of you have thought that you were individuals separate and distinct from each other and from me, looking upon the difficulties and the suffering of others as if these were something outside yourselves.

62. I can carry all your burdens, because I know that my Father takes care of me, and if you are weary then my Father will take care of you as He takes care of me.

63. He has given me power to overcome all conditions, and this power is manifested in you also. Therefore do not look upon others as separate from yourselves and from me, but feel with me in the whole of humanity. Feel with me and you shall know me, and what you do for others you do for me.

64. Therefore you shall not weary in doing things for

the Love of God when you know me and know that my Father is your Father also.

65. Regard not the work done as the greatest, but the Love in which it is performed.

66. The majority of people look upon their achievements with self-esteem and will say, " I have built this, I have built that ; I have created this, and I have created that." No one creates anything separate from God, for it is God that gave you power to do so. There is no outside of God, for He is Infinite in nature.

67. Therefore recognise that the source of power is Love, and that it comes through the Christ within ; then regard not the work as the greatest, but the love by which it is performed. All things will pass away but Love remains forever.

68. Your mind is the mirror of your soul, and even in your suffering you will grow stronger, knowing that you are always in the presence of the Father.

69. Your heart and your imagination are closely related. What is in your heart, so does your imagination reproduce.

70. These talks that I am giving you are bringing your heart nearer to the source of all Life.

71. I know that some have complained to the brother that they have not been allowed to come in to hear these talks. This work can only be done under special conditions, and I have chosen you—you have not chosen me.

72. It is not because I want to close others out from these great truths ; remember that. The reason is that you have been chosen. Many have been called but few have been chosen. I taught my disciples in secret, so that they could understand the Power of God and how to use it wisely. In this way I also teach you, so that you can also use this power wisely to bring about a better understanding in the world.

73. When you go forth into the world you shall be my disciples, spreading the truth of the everlasting Life, telling that Love alone is the ruling power, and that this power alone can bring peace and happiness into the world.

74. Man must look unto me ; in this way he can raise himself up. As the serpent was raised in the wilderness by Moses, so is the son of man raised up.

75. Then let the Christ abide in your heart and you will be conscious of ever fresh unfoldment. You will see, hear, and know the creative power of the Spirit of God personified in the Christ of God in you.

76. Real prayer is deep earnestness ; it has great attractive power, and I want to impress upon your mind the importance of being earnest in prayer, not to an outside God but communion with the Father through the Christ of God within.

(THE SCRIBE'S REMARKS :

A deep silence is felt and the Auditorium is filled with Light.)

77. That is what I mean by being earnest in prayer. The answer is : The Creative Power and the place of creation are within ; there I dwell, then think of me as living in All.

78. When you love me you love my Father also. The Father has great things in store for those who love Him.

79. I am the Word that was in the beginning with God, and everything came to be by my hand, and without me not even one thing came to be.

80. It was the Father who created through me ; He is speaking through me now.

81. No one has ever seen God, yet I am in the bosom of my Father who is God. He has declared me and you have heard Him.

82. I am the seed of my Father in Heaven which He has replanted and will bring forth the same fruit in all of you.

83. The truth of the brotherhood of man is beginning to show its growth above the darkness of the earth. It is beginning to pierce the mind of man, and truly I say it is still the purpose of the Christ to fulfil the purpose of God.

84. Therefore what I have been sent forth to do shall be fulfilled. The purpose of God is fulfilled through the Christ of God in all. Please remember what I say to you !

85. I am one with humanity—in the Garden of Humanity one of the first blooms ; and I shall be with you all days, even unto the end of the world.

86. There is no separation between us, and when you leave your earthly tenement, and come into the inner realms of consciousness, I shall still be with you, and you shall be conscious of a greater understanding ; you will be conscious of a greater love, a love in which all enmity is dissolved away.

87. In my Father's house there is Divine Love, and all who turn to my Father in repentance receive His love, and My Father will overwhelm them with His bounties.

88. There are many mansions in my Father's House ; these are grades of consciousness. The greatest hindrance to the expression of the Divine is ignorance of the Christ in you.

89. Who is the greatest sinner ? Can you condemn another and not condemn yourself ? Think !

90. Many who have lived on earth in ignorance, mis-understanding their power, used it wrongly, because they did not understand the Infinite Love of God. But now they are growing and unfolding into freedom, through understanding and love.

91. All memories of the past are being dissolved away, yet through these experiences they have come to know the

love of God. As the heart rejoices in the beauty of the Love of the Father, so does the soul bloom forth in all its glory.

92. The Spirit of God in man is awakening to the truth of Its everlasting Divine Life of Love and happiness, joyfully expressing Itself in Its true nature, Love.

93. As the truth of Being is unfolded in the mind, so will man discard the divisions in the limited forms of religion. Then there will be one truth, one people of God, one flock and one shepherd, and all will listen to my Voice.

94. The darkness that surrounds you, which seems to oppose you, is the means of my growth in you. Fear not, for I am the conqueror.

95. And when you encounter sorrow and difficulties, greet them with joy, for through them you will grow in me by overcoming them.

96. God's Idea is His Word, and I am that Word, was born in the flesh, blossomed therein, grew out of the flesh to live forever with my Father, and this is the way of all humanity.

97. Therefore I manifest in the innermost plane of being as I always did. My roots are in the Eternal Mind of God.

98. The Word was in the beginning—the Word was with God ; that very word was God, and that Word was made flesh. It grew out of the flesh triumphant, overcoming the flesh, overcoming the world. This the Christ grows and blooms forth in the image and likeness of God, for the Christ is the seed of God planted in the world to overcome the world.

99. Therefore I manifest in the innermost plane of Being. I knew there could be no such thing as death, for this existed only in the limited mind of man. When you can grasp the wonderful truth of the Eternal Life, that Life Itself is not affected by so-called death.

100. There is no interruption in Life by the experience of so-called death, yet there is release from the hindrances of the flesh by the unfoldment of the Spirit.

101. Some have come from the earth-plane hating their brothers and sisters. These hates melt away and dissolve into nothingness by true understanding. The Spirit becomes more and more the Life of God, recognise at once that the lower planes of manifestation are but a lower state of consciousness in which Life manifests. Your work is to bring the Kingdom of Heaven on earth.

102. You must consciously discern that which prevents growth and unfoldment, and not until you consciously become aware of the " One " Consciousness existing in all, does freedom come. You cannot move out of the lower into the higher until this becomes known to you.

103. My Father remembers nothing against you, neither shall you remember anything against your brother or your sister, so be at peace now, for now is Eternity.

104. The Divine man is complete in God. He passes through all the stages of growth until the consciousness realises its true source.

105. Then the Divine man realises his omnipotence in the Reality of God.

106. All who are looking with me upon those who are growing on earth are filled with the longing for the will of the Father to be fulfilled.

107. By experiences you overcome your difficulties and you see how much power is dammed up because of your beliefs, your hatreds, your ignorance in the world. We long for the will of God to be fulfilled in mankind to see the wonderful power of Love expressed.

108. The end is in the beginning and the beginning is in the end. The end of all separation is in God, by understanding His true nature, and the expression of His Infinite Divine Love.

109. Is there anyone among you who, having an hundred sheep, if one of them should get lost, would not leave the ninety and nine and go in search for the one which is lost until it is found ?

110. And, when it is found, rejoice and carry it back to the fold, so that the fold would be complete ?

111. I say to you that there is more joy in Heaven over one who repenteth, than over ninety-nine that need no repentance.

112. My Father is complete ; not one can ever be lost, all shall be found, and brought back to the fold and there shall be rejoicing, because the fold will be complete. This is the will of God—complete happiness and peace with Love for each one.

113. This peace will come, for it is already ordained.

114. The Father's idea for the world is perfection and nothing less. As the Spirit of God is personified as the Christ in you, so shall the Christ reign in the glory in which His Father created him.

115. Many have passed from the earth still clinging to the false idea that matter is a reality in itself. This age-long sense-belief has retarded the progress of many deeply reverent and noble souls. They still live in the material sense as it is still real to them.

116. Remember, what you see is not a Reality ; it is but the reflection of something within. That which is seen on the surface will change and pass away and dissolve into nothingness, but that which is Real shall remain.

117. Do not look upon material things as real ; they are only the effects of that which is unseen. Many have come into the inner realm with the idea of the solidity or reality of matter.

118. Although noble souls, believing, yet they are asleep in Christ, not awakened to the understanding of the power of the Christ and the freedom of the Christ Life.

These noble souls are hindered by their limited beliefs and lack understanding of the true nature of things.

119. This prevents them from unfolding to the higher experiences in store for them.

120. The only substance is God. All is in His Mind, all is His creation. The visible is but the reflection of His ideas, the real being permanently, everlastingly rooted in His Eternal Reality.

121. Give this your deep contemplation until it becomes real in your own consciousness.

122. Set earnestly about this work, and if you do it as you ought be assured that you will soon find the effects of it in your life.

123. Thus the Christ is risen.

MY PEACE AND MY LOVE I LEAVE WITH YOU TO REMAIN WITH YOU.

Now we will enter into the Sanctuary together.
Each one of you look towards me.

SILENCE

MY PEACE, MY LOVE REMAINS WITH YOU.

———

(THE SCRIBE'S REMARKS:

The Master blessed us all in his usual way, and his peace and his love remained with us.)

TALK 13

YOU ARE THE BRANCH ON THE VINE THAT BEARS MY FRUIT

My love, my peace I bring to you.

1. See the Life of God as the " Christ Consciousness " in you, " I am the Life " is then realised.

2. Life is consciousness. It is God who is expressing Himself. There can be no other. The Christ is the only begotten Son of the Father.

3. The great man is the Christ who rules the world in which everything exists. This Christ-man also exists in every individual, and there is no separation anywhere! If you can realise this, then you will see how wonderful it is to understand the wholeness of Reality where there is no separation, no distinction.

4. The growth of the Divine Seed is manifesting in you. The hidden work is going on. Wait patiently ; and as the fruit in season cometh, so shall the Christ in you blossom forth as the Fruit of God, the finished product.

5. There is a continual work going on within each of you, even if you do not realise it. The great truth is, there is no standing still ; there is movement everywhere, continuously and upward, in the whole of humanity. This is the Christ working in you.

6. Yes, in answer to your question, when these talks with you are complete they will be printed, so that the world can have them also.

7. Spiritual Forces are now being used for the purpose of bringing higher knowledge and wisdom to the world as they did thousands of years ago. It is in the mind of man where we find separation and distinction. But the Christ the Spirit of God remains the same always and is the seed

that is forcing Its way through the darkness of the human mind.

8. The earth is the substance surrounding the seed of the plant ; so is humanity the substance surrounding the Spirit of God. Mankind is growing to maturity, and will become conscious of the indwelling Spirit as the only Reality.

9. The best way to help this great work is to close the door of the senses, for when thine eye is single thy whole body will be full of light.

10. It is the inner vision that sees this mighty Power unfolding its beauty and Intelligence, which is Omnipresent, expressing itself wholly and not separate from the whole, but the whole expressing Itself in the many, and the many existing in the whole. There is no separation anywhere, please remember this. This must take root in your mind. It is the pillars upon which the rock of Truth stands.

11. The consciousness of God envelops everything, and everything is within His consciousness, so His Consciousness in you will reveal His image and likeness.

12. Listen to the beat of your heart and realise the full stream of the Life of God pulsating through it. In reality you are one with the Heart of Christ in the Father.

13. God rejoices to pour Himself out through the channels He has prepared for this purpose.

14. You are the channels He is preparing, and soon you will feel the urge. That I have come to you is no mere chance but is the unfoldment of the Spirit which underlies the whole of humanity. The call never goes unanswered. It is the great Crusade of the Christ that dwells in you that is forcing its way into your consciousness. The inner shall be expressed in the outer, and the outer shall become the inner ; then man is matured by the Spirit of Christ.

15. The world shall know him as he lives the Life, and the lamb and the lion shall lie down together. The lamb

of God is the great Power within man ; the lion is the man of the senses, unruly, not knowing himself, but he is subdued by the Lamb of God, the Christ within. Love overcomes all things. Love is God, and God is Love.

16. This pulsating Life delights Itself in you when you delight yourself in It.

17. God is omnipresent and eternal, and you are with Him. To become like Him you must know there can be no separation, no distinction.

18. Perhaps you do not quite comprehend what I mean when I say " no separation, no distinction." When you see distinction you are living in separation, you are living in the personality of the senses. It is when you are living in separation that you see distinction, and seeing distinction you feel separation ; and this is the great illusion.

19. Distinction is a product of the mind, but you will note that there is no distinction in the Christ of God, there is no distinction in the Spirit of God in you. In each and every one of you there is the same Spirit. In that Spirit you have power, for nothing can assail it. Become aware of It now in your lives and be free. This is the freedom of the Truth, the Truth that sets you free.

20. Only in your belief in separation do you have distinction, and so you feel separation. Thus you must discern all that causes separation before you can know me.

21. Open your eyes and see God everywhere. This consciousness of God is spreading all over the earth as each one feels himself or herself one with the " One " Heart pulsating with Love.

22. In the heart of God there is everlasting Love and the Christ is one with the heart of God, and this Christ is the Saviour of the Race.

23. There is but one Christ in the creation of the world and everything exists by Him, and nothing that ever was made could have been made without Him, and by Him

you came into Being. This is the Son, the only begotten Son of God, the one Christ, the great Divine man in Whom you all move and have your Being, and He moves in each and every one of you.

24. This Divine Christ is the conscious expression of the Father. He is conscious of all things, conscious of the power to create, conscious of all things existing in the world, conscious of Himself in each and every individual, and there is no separation in Him.

25. Think then of this one holy Divine man existing in each and every one of you. He is male and female complete in Himself.

26. Before you can know Him you must rid yourselves of false beliefs in separation, beliefs that breed hatred, beliefs that have no foundation in Me.

27. You can have no separate beliefs when you realise the Truth of the one Eternal Living Spirit that is manifesting now in you and me. Can you now follow any belief that separates you from your brothers and sisters?

28. Do not cling too hard to the earthly life, for it is but a preparatory step in the growth of the Christ in you.

29. Many are holding too strongly to the earthly life and the things that exist in it.

30. Use these things wisely, but do not cling to them, and do not allow them to cling to you. They are for your use, to prepare you for further unfoldment, to greater strength, power and glory.

31. Be not afraid; you lose nothing that is real. Christ is your only Reality and is the Eternal Son of God.

32. No love is ever lost. It is the expression of God and pours through the garment that shrouds it.

33. When you begin to realise this, all on earth will know that It is the Love of God that is expressing Itself through the soul. The body is the garment through which the Life is expressed in the physical.

34. You must not despise this garment but consecrate it to Christ, realising the mighty power that is within. And as you consecrate this garment to the Christ, so shall it become as the inner and the inner becomes the outer. Thus ye are born again, this time not of the flesh nor of the will of man, but of the Spirit of God. For I have said, " Call no man your father on earth, for one is your Father who is in heaven."

35. Rejoice and have no fear. Fear is but the dimmed sight that prevents you from seeing clearly. It clouds your Spiritual vision, yet only for a time, for freedom comes through the Eternal Christ in you.

36. All fear is dispelled by Love, for Love casteth out fear. The fear of evil, the fear of man, the fear of God, are all products of the material sense and have no foundation in Reality.

37. The Love of God sets you free from all these fears that separate you from His Divine Presence.

38. Therefore fear neither man nor beast ; neither must you fear God, but love Him. When this true nature of the Christ is revealed in your own consciousness, there is the power that Daniel had in the den of lions. This power is yours also.

39. Nothing on earth or in the heavens can overcome you, in the recognition of the fact that this Christ, the Spirit of God in you, is all power in Itself and is the Creative Principle behind all things existing in heaven and on earth. When you realise this, you will not be afraid.

40. The lowest are seeking God in some way or another. As my disciples it is your work to show them the true path through Love and by example. Not by mere words, but by kindness, by love, by understanding.

41. Most people fear the experience called death. But when you pass through this experience you find yourself

to be a living, breathing soul more alive than ever before, for it is the soul that breathes, not the body.

42. Death is but the gateway to the greater expansion of the Christ, the flower that grows and blooms in God, and when you find yourselves living, breathing souls more alive than ever before, it overwhelms you. The one wish is, that you want to return to your loved ones to tell them of the wonderful truth of the glory that you have found.

43. Many have returned to you but your ears are deaf and your eyes are blind. All must pass through the same experience and this is the joy of those who have already passed through the experience called death. This joy which all will experience is beyond the understanding of mortal sense.

44. You become more conscious of the freedom of Life, because the soul breathes beyond the flesh.

45. The body is the Temple of the Spirit. Spirit Life is eternal. You find that all you thought true becomes a reality.

46. In your minds you have pictured the experience of seeing loved ones again, and know them face to face ; this I truly tell you is real. Even those who injured you and those you also injured through ignorance will rejoice at meeting you again.

47. This is the eternal law of the Spirit, the unfoldment of the Christ. As the consciousness becomes aware of this inner life, a change takes place in the consciousness, and all these hatreds disappear. Then it is wise for you to understand this while on earth.

48. Some born in ignorance die in ignorance. Now this shall not be your fate. The mist dissolves away, and there remains the beauty of the Christ of God.

49. When I talk of the Christ of God I know that you are beginning to understand what the Christ means, It is the great Divine Man of God. Christ is the Divine Man on

earth which includes all human souls. As cells exist in the one body, so does each one of you exist in the Christ of God. The seed of God is in you and it is sure to grow to maturity.

50. No greater joy can ever be experienced than when that which you vaguely thought true becomes a Reality. You find that you have lost nothing but all is gained with a new understanding.

51. You will be overwhelmed by the unlimited sense that takes hold of you, while all the false beliefs will drop from you.

52. You will be the same living soul, no matter in which way you leave your body. You are still you ; and in all those you loved, you will find a greater love and a greater attraction, a greater understanding, for nothing in love is lost.

53. Did I not show my hands and feet to my disciples ? I was the same they knew on earth. Yet I knew that I was the Christ of God, and it is for every one of you also to realise this Truth, for through the realisation of it comes " awareness "—a conscious awareness that ignorance cannot destroy.

54. Ignorance clouds the Reality in you. Most people are slow to learn because of false beliefs.

55. Then forget all error and ignorance and enter fully into the truth of your Being now.

56. Can you fully enter into this now ? You are living beings. It is the Life of God that lives in you ; as a living being, you exist in God and not outside Him. When this is understood there is an expansion of the consciousness, an awareness of Reality, an awareness of an Eternal Reality that exists, having no end. Oh, would you know this ! It would set you free now.

57. Even my disciples did not understand fully until I reappeared to them.

58. The eternal Christ of God liveth for ever. Yet they could not quite understand ; they were just people like yourselves, but through the Spirit of the Christ they became my Apostles.

59. Even now I know that many of you here do not fully understand that it is I who speak to you.

60. Neither did Thomas believe. He, too, wanted to see my hands and feet and thrust his hand into my side before he would believe.

61. It was eight days afterwards when all my disciples gathered together and Thomas was with them. I took his hand and put it into my side and showed my hands and feet. Thomas was overcome and exclaimed, " My Lord, my God."

62. He was overwhelmed with the realisation that, after the experience called death, one still lived, and in this is the secret of power in all, yet few could fully understand it.

63. In the realisation of this dwells the power of the Christ in you. That is why I made it the greatest point in my work. It shows that this world is but a preparatory step in the unfoldment of the Christ within. This realisation is what you also require, then all power will be given unto you in heaven and on earth.

64. Thomas believed because he had seen. But I say blessed are those who have not seen me, and have believed.

65. That into which God has breathed the breath of His Life can never be dead. Only the dead who believe in death bury their dead. The living Christ does not die.

66. If you could turn your eyes inward and see what I am looking at now through these eyes, you would gain a greater understanding.

67. Yes, your eyes will see and your ears will hear with a new understanding of the Living Christ of God.

68. Those who are weary and tired will rest as they have never rested before.

69. Those who have suffered while on earth and have passed through the Gate of their Gethsemane, some aged perhaps, and infirm, with a memory of their condition while on earth, will find that it is just an image in the mind that requires discarding. Nevertheless, the soul is scarred for the time being. They pass into a deep slumber, the soul sleeps, then wakens in the Reality of the Christ ; they are rejuvenated and freed from all conditions that scarred the memory.

70. Yet, if they liked, they could reproduce a condition to show those on earth who they were. But immediately they return into the inner, they discard these conditions and live in the realisation of the Christ the Perfection of God.

71. It is sometimes hard to make those living on earth believe the truth that the Everlasting Christ which dwells in each and every one is the Father Himself.

72. Then those who are weary and tired will rest as they have never rested before. And when they awaken they will find that the best and the highest that could ever be realised is true.

73. Your loved ones are not afar off, but present with you, as they have always been since they left you, but your material sense blinds you to their presence.

74. Oh, how you will try to help those you have loved and left behind, yet all this is in store for all. This is the great relief that you feel. Yet it pains you to see how ignorant the world is about the Reality of Life.

75. My words will bring to your consciousness the realisation of the truth of Reality—that you are also eternal because you live in Reality. You live and move and have your being in Him who created you and He lives in you.

76. You will then begin your further unfoldment, which is never ceasing—with it a greater understanding of God, a greater love of God, a greater realisation of His wonderful Universe in which you live and move and have your being.

77. If I could imprint in your minds now all that exists, you would be free of all fear and doubt.

78. The greatest thing of all is " Love "—Love that has no beginning and no ending. It is ever pouring Itself out, and, as you are caught up in Its opulence, so do you love as the Christ of God that has risen.

79. The Father unfolds in you His love, and the Christ is this love in you.

80. I long for you to know of this indwelling Christ in you, so that you can understand that there is no separation between us.

81. In My Father's house there are many mansions. These are the varying degrees of consciousness. A consciousness unfolds, so does it manifest that which it unfolds.

82. As unfoldment takes place through the consciousness it manifests what it unfolds. What is realised is seen and understood. Your consciousness is the means through which the Christ of God manifests, unfolding the greater beyond.

83. The Christ of God is incarnate and dwells within, nearer than hands and feet, and can hear even before you ask.

84. When you ask in faith, understanding that the place of creation is in you, there is nothing that the Father will not do for you if you ask Him in my name. Then ask in the name of the Christ of God that is within you. I will hear you and what you ask will be done unto you.

85. For you are the branches on the vine that bears my

fruit : yes, capable of abundant fruit. With me you can do all things ; without me you can do nothing.

86. I of myself am nothing ; it is the Spirit of the Father within me that speaketh ; He doeth all these things and more.

87. I am behind all thought and speech and am omnipresent, and my Love is the key to all knowledge, wisdom and power.

88. My love unfolds your consciousness in the inner realm, and, as Love unfolds in you, so do you know more of me.

89. Even if you speak with eloquence and have not love in your heart, you are but a tinkling cymbal.

90. Even if you acquire all knowledge and practise a faith that can do all things, yet without Love in your heart, what you do does not profit you.

91. Should you give alms to the less fortunate and feed the poor, yet without love, you have done nothing.

92. Love is not understood ; It is kind and suffers injustice without rebuke.

93. Love does not return evil for evil, but good for evil. In the meek, Love guides them in good judgment.

94. Love is all power, yet is humble. Love does not make vain displays, nor does it boast of its accomplishments.

95. Love never fails, because Love is God and God is Love.

96. The Divine Stream of Love flows into your heart when your Heart beats with the Heart of Love. Peace comes into your mind, and your soul radiates the true nature of our Father in heaven.

97. I enjoy speaking to my Father who is Love ! His Love casteth out all fear ; no harm can come nigh you with His Love in your heart. Be at peace then, and know that I am with you.

98. Love is always in the midst, and dwells in the kindly darkness that surrounds you.

99. Be not afraid of this darkness, for I am the Light that overcometh the darkness. Yet the darkness does not comprehend the Light, for the Light alone comprehendeth.

100. The darkness is but a shadow in the mind, yet through it and by it the Christ blooms into power and glory. Become aware of this power, and all conditions will pass from you. Shrink not from responsibilities nor from any task, even if it be a cross. You will find joy in the unfoldment by overcoming, because *you* will know you are the light of the world that overcometh the darkness.

101. It is the Light that comprehendeth ; the darkness comprehendeth not. Where the Light is, darkness disappears.

102. The soul that seeks nourishment from the Christ within becomes strong. It is the house that is built upon the Rock of Truth that nothing can assail from without.

103. Seek my Silent Love that dwells within you. Love all, bless all with Love, and I shall bless you a hundredfold.

104. For I delight in you when you bless with Love. I am working in you when you love, and when you bless with love I am by your side, for I am love.

105. Do not seek gain or reward for your love, nor make show of your love before men, but Love in secret. Do all things that come to thy hand for the Love of God, not to please men.

106. You are the future, the past and the present. Learn this at once, so that I can work in you now ; then all which is unreal will be swept into the abyss where it belongs.

107. You are all just where you ought to be to do this work, and God cannot fail when you are alive with

Christ, for you are the Branch on the Vine that bears My Fruit.

Now we will enter into the Sanctuary. Look towards me.

SILENCE

MY PEACE, MY LOVE I LEAVE WITH YOU TO REMAIN WITH YOU.

———————

(THE SCRIBE'S REMARKS :

A beautiful purple light filled the hall as the silence was in progress, and as the Master left there was a sense of love and peace which cannot be described in words.)

TALK 14

I am the Good Shepherd and my Sheep Know my Voice

My peace, my blessings I bring to you to remain with you.

1. Now is a wonderful time for you all, for you are growing naturally into the Christ of God, your true Spiritual existence.

2. Even your body will be brought into tune with the Higher Law. You do not become your own idea ; you are God's Idea.

3. The great Truth is that no one can alter or change the Idea of God. It is designed to bloom forth, to come to maturity. Nothing can hinder its progress. That which seemingly hinders the expression of the Divine Idea is not a hindrance but a means of gaining experience.

4. Do not be afraid of the world, because the world cannot conquer you, but the power of the Christ within you conquers the world. All conditions should be looked upon as experience ; then you will grow out of them stronger. You will also know that your strength comes from within and not from without. This strength is always with you ; It is the power of the Christ of God.

5. This cannot fail, for you have opened the way to the Higher Law through the recognition of the Christ of God in you.

6. Immediately you recognise the Christ of God as the only Reality, the Reality which is eternal and ever-present, you enter into the higher law that is being expressed through you by your recognition of this Truth. When this Truth is not recognised, there is what we call the natural law, and every person is subject unto it. But

when the higher law supersedes the natural law, It has power over nature ; this is the Christ that is within you.

7. Recognise this higher law now through the recognition of the Christ of God as the Creator of all things in heaven and on earth, and through Him all things came into being. The word that is with God, the word that is God, and this word became flesh manifesting in your midst. Thus the word of God moves in and through you ; this is the Truth of the everlasting Life, the Life that is eternal.

8. Say in your heart with Love and understanding, " Thy Will be done in me " and the Christ will move in you, for Christ is God Manifested in the flesh.

9. The Christ is God manifesting in the flesh. I repeat this, so that it will sink into your minds. By recognising and realising this Truth a tremendous force rises with you : the Christ is God manifesting in you now.

10. Your innermost and highest thought is in the consciousness of the Absolute.

11. Therefore the higher the thought, the more power it has. Thy will be done in me. It is God's will that is manifesting in me now. No heavenly or earthly being can alter the will of the Father. It is paramount ; in this understanding the consciousness becomes aware of the highest, the innermost thought of the Absolute. Thy Will be done in me.

12. In this lies the great power in heaven and on earth.

13. This is the power that will dissolve away all discord, all that is not of Itself true.

14. Your treasure is where your heart is, and your treasure should be the continual outpicturing of the Truth of the Christ, " I and the Father are One."

15. Think then deeply of this truth, for it is the concentrated light in your own consciousness, a light that is

being expressed in your soul by means of the Christ in you, " I and the Father are one." It is the Father's will, that you shall express Him in all His glory, in all His power, in all His Wisdom, in all His Love.

16. Do not repeat my sayings like mere platitudes ; read them again and again, as if saying them in earnest prayer.

17. When you pray there must be a deep feeling of reverence, and a closing of the outer ; then, you enter into the inner. As you pray, feel your oneness with Him Who created you within Himself.

18. If you repeat my sayings with understanding in this manner you will have many things revealed to you.

·19. The inner voice will speak to you, the inner sight will be open to you. In this tabernacle of God there is the Golden Silence of Love that protects you from all conditioning, a silence that brings you into the presence of the Almighty.

20. Then the unreal, the shadow, will disappear and the real will reveal Itself in you.

21. I am indeed glad to have been with you for this short session in earnest teaching. Do not look upon me as afar off and separated from you.

22. That which has happened in the past you relegate to your memory, but things of the past are with you in the present. Then be consciously aware of the presence of God, the Christ, that is always with you. You can create only in the present, never in the past or the future : only in the Eternal Now.

23. Your enjoyment in my presence can be continuous and so can you learn of me, by your constant thought of my presence with you.

24. My words are Life to you. Believe in me, and have courage ; your very desire to help, when really unselfish, is already done.

25. The desire to help must come from the heart. In your heart you will find there a Presence that will come forth and will express Itself in you and through you, and your desire will be fulfilled.

26. Remember that there can be *no* separation when you desire to help and the desire that comes from the heart it is done immediately because your Father heareth ; He is the Servant of all.

27. You have victory over all things through the Christ within.

28. The Christ is God's Eternal Son manifested in the human race. In this understanding you reach the highest possible while in the flesh.

29. While living in the flesh you recognise that there are influences of the flesh. But these influences are not evil influences ; they are the means through which you obtain the understanding of things.

30. You grow out of these conditions just as a seed, when planted in the ground, grows and blooms, and also brings forth its seed ; so does the Spirit of God do the same in you. The Spirit of God is not always confined to the flesh ; It grows out of the mortal conditions into the immortal, as it always was immortal. The Life in the body is in no way separated from the totality of all Life.

31. Study my sayings and the veil will be lifted from your eyes ; the son of man waits with you, to overcome your belief in separation.

32. There is freedom in Christ, yet Christ lives in the human race as the Eternal Son of God. This mighty power will harmonise all beings into the one family. The Spirit in each and every soul shall recognise the source of its being.

33. In the recognition of this there is freedom. The inner being expressed in the outer, this is " Thy Will be done on earth as it is in heaven."

34. Man is hurt by man again and again, and not until man is crucified through his own folly will he open his eyes to the great " Oneness " of all through the Christ of God.

35. I do not speak of myself ; It is the Father who ever remains in me, who is the Father of all, and is all. It is He that speaketh in me and for me. The same Life in the Father is in the son.

36. Let the sense of personalities pass from your mind ; then you will see the glory of God, His only begotten Son that reigneth forever.

37. Personalities are but the mask that is put on from outside, and as long as you hold on to personalities so will you live in illusion.

38. So many are dwelling on the personality of Jesus, with the result that they fail to see the eternal Christ in all. For this I have come to tell you, so that ye shall know that the Christ of God is universal.

39. Your work is to co-operate with Christ, so that you may be avenues for healing in all manner of ways.

40. Realise that Spirit is the only Reality. This Spirit vitalises your soul and body, and is the only power there is. You live and move and have your being in God, and God lives in you. It is God Himself who is expressing Himself. To know this fully, means freedom in your life now. This is the way to the Truth of the everlasting Life. " Know ye not I am in the Father and the Father is in me."

41. The forgiveness of God is spontaneous, and instantaneously all errors are blotted out by the inflow of His Everlasting Love. Then do not hinder the Divine gift by regrets, sadness or remorse.

42. With this understanding the love of God flows into the heart that opens to It ; this then is made manifest in the flesh. If you are sad in remorse, having regrets, your

mind is filled with shadows, but when the Love of God fills you, there is no room for shadows, they dissolve away.

43. The only condition is, that you open yourselves to Him so that He may fill you full with His everlasting Love.

44. Blessed are the merciful, for in them I will abide.

45. Rejoice, for your reward is increased in Heaven. Heaven is not a place outside yourselves ; heaven is within you, and this reward is increased from within. Your reward is immediate and goes with you, increasing into eternity.

46. In you the Light of the World shineth ; then let the Light be seen by your actions and not by mere words.

47. Words can deceive the mind of the untutored but actions reveal the nature of the individual. From the heart you must speak and feel.

48. Thus you will glorify your Father which is in Heaven. The Kingdom of Heaven is within you. How wonderful is the Truth when it is understood—" I and the Father are one."

49. You are those that hath been spoken of as the people of God—a people among all peoples with no allegiances except to God the Father of all nations, and to His son the Christ, this only begotten Son that dwelleth in all souls.

50. To be my disciples you must be Universal. There can be no allegiances except to God. Any other allegiances limit the true expression of God the Father in you.

51. Then even if you say to your brother " You are a nursemaid," " You are a fool," you are guilty of trespassing against the Law of Love.

52. And when thou prayest to your Father in Heaven, firstly remember those who have a grievance against you. Become reconciled in your heart to them, then your Father will hear you.

53. Only when in your heart you are reconciled is there freedom and forgiveness ; then your heart will express its true nature, and God the Father who is Love will bless you.

54. For in your heart is the key to the entrance of my Father's house where bounties are stored up for you.

55. Do not add deceptive words ; they count for nothing—these words are not heard in the Father's realm. To say something that you do not mean, something that you do not feel, is not prayer.

56. If you will remember my words when you pray you will pray from your heart in secret, forgiving and forgiven, for I know the power of God that dwells in the hearts of all who Love me.

57. If you speak with the Will of God all is possible, and your word will not return unto you void but will accomplish that which it is sent forth to do. Think then where the power of God dwells.

58. Let your heart be pure, so that it can speak with me, for I do the Will of my Father.

59. Many are kind to their friends and hate their enemies, but I have no enemies, all are my friends, and to be like me you must do likewise.

60. No one is your enemy when you love enough. When you recognise this, you will see how true it is. When selfishness and ignorance dissolve away, Love which is Truth is manifested. There ·can be no enemies in the Father's House of Love ; all must dwell in Love and Peace, otherwise you cannot enter in. To enter heaven you must bring heaven with you.

61. God loves His most disobedient child ; therefore love also those who do you an injustice, so that you may become as your Father which is in Heaven. It is the Father that speaketh in me. These words have been recorded so that you will remember them, so that they will remain with you.

62. When the word is spoken and you hear it, it lasts for a while, but when it is recorded it will bring back to your memory the meaning and the way that my words were spoken.

63. For if you love only those who love you, there is little gain ; but if you love those who hate you, then there is great reward.

64. Love turneth away wrath, and the powers of ignorance can in no way harm you.

65. Salute your brother, no matter what position he may be in ; he may be greater in Heaven, even if less on earth.

66. Salute all those who salute you, for truly I tell you this, that many who are lesser on earth are greater in heaven. It is well that you should know this now, for the time will come when you will see the glory of God expressed through the simple and the wise.

67. In this way you become perfect as your Father in Heaven is perfect.

68. Do not give alms and then blow a trumpet as to thy goodness ; rather let not your left hand know what your right hand is doing.

69. For whatever is done from the heart your Father knoweth and rewards you generously.

70. When you pray to your Father in Heaven, you must enter into Heaven by closing the doors of the senses that lead to the outer.

71. For only in the heart of hearts where there is the Golden Silence of Love can your prayers be truly heard.

72. Then enter into the Heart of God through your own heart with pure thought, unselfish and free, leaving all that pertains to the outer, outside.

73. Remember thy Purity is in me, the Christ of God.

74. Ask for forgiveness, not as a servant would, but as a child would ask of its parent, knowing well that that

forgiveness was already given by the heart that loves it.

75. Peter asked how many times a disciple should forgive : seven times ? Is it not written that my word said seven times seventy. That means eternal forgiveness. Your Father in Heaven forgives you in His heart the moment you ask for forgiveness. It must be the same with you.

76. For thy Father knoweth what is in thy heart, and He knows what you are in need of.

77. Therefore pray in this manner in your heart.

78. Our Father in Heaven, Thy name is hallowed, Thy Kingdom come.

79. Let Thy will be done, as in Heaven so on earth.

80. Give us bread for our needs from day to day.

81. And forgive us our offences as we forgive our offenders.

82. And do not let us enter into temptation but deliver us from error. Because thine is the Kingdom and the Power and the Glory for ever and ever. Amen.

83. Memorise and repeat this prayer in your heart. Say it every day of your life and you will find a tremendous source of power, wisdom and love entering into you. The Father will speak through you ; He will express Himself in you, in His Love, Wisdom and Power.

84. Your Father in Heaven has already forgiven your faults when you forgive others their faults.

85. But if you do not forgive in your own heart there can be no forgiveness. In the heart is the meeting place of God and man ; you can meet Him face to face when you have forgiven all.

86. Then what shall ye say, if in your heart you have not forgiven your brother ?

87. What shall you say when you meet your Father face to face ? He knoweth what is in your heart.

88. Neither should you cherish things of the world more than the things of the Spirit.

89. The treasures of the Spirit are lasting, while the treasures of the world are fleeting and unstable.

90. I do not deny you the things of the world, but you should know that the things of the Spirit are everlasting.

91. Where your treasure is, there your heart will be also.

92. The eye is the window of the soul; then let it be not confused or diseased, for if the soul is dark so will the body express that darkness.

93. Do not worry over what you will eat or drink nor what your body will wear. Life is much more important than all these other things.

94. In Life all things exist; your Father in Heaven is the good Provider; He provides for all His creatures, and you are much more, you are His children and you are my disciples.

95. All things grow because of Him who created all, because He exists in all He created.

96. God is not separate and apart from His creation. He exists in His creation, and His creation exists in Him. If God did not exist in you, you could not be alive because there is no life apart from God, and if you did not exist in God He could not be Infinite.

97. Your Father knows all the things that are necessary for you, and all these things shall be given unto you.

98. Firstly seek the Kingdom of God, the source of all things, and everything shall be yours.

99. The only condition is a pure heart, and the ability to receive.

100. When you examine these words of mine you will see the mighty truth that is in them.

101. Thus the simple and the wise are caught up in the stream of the Father's love and become channels for the

expression of all that He has. What is mine is Thine and what is Thine is mine.

102. Remember I am always with you and know that the nails in my hands and feet will still ache until all shall return unto me, for I am the good Shepherd and all my sheep know my voice.

103. Great work has been done in your midst, and though you have not been aware of it you have helped greatly towards it. It was for this that I have come among you. I have drawn you together, I have brought you into my presence, I have linked you up with the great Spiritual Forces that surround you, and the protection of my Father is about you.

104. The brother whom I have overshadowed, his consciousness has been increased in value, and you will find that his work in the future will be even greater than it has been in the past.

105. I am always present with you, do not think that I am leaving you now and going afar from you, think of me as the ever-present in your midst.

MY PEACE, MY LOVE I HAVE BROUGHT TO YOU WILL REMAIN WITH YOU.

Now we will enter into the Sanctuary of the Silent Healing Power. Just look towards me.

SILENCE

I thank you, Father—now I ascend to Thee.

(THE SCRIBE'S REMARKS:

A bright light was visible, while music and bells were heard, as the Master took his departure from the brother. This light filled the whole hall and a tremendous power was felt. All passed out of the Auditorium and not a word was spoken.

Nothing has been added, nor has anything been taken away from the words spoken by the Master ; they are just as they were given. A truly wonderful demonstration of the fact that the Master is still with us.)

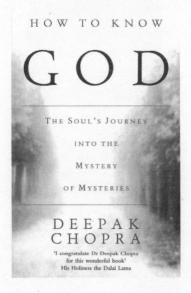

Guide to the Soul

by Patrick Harpur

Author of *The Philosophers' Secret Fire*

Who am I?

What's my life's purpose?

Where am I going when I die?

These questions lie at the heart of all our lives, yet clear answers seem hard to come by. *A Complete Guide to the Soul* explains that answers can be found in a secret history that runs like quicksilver through Western culture, from philosophy and alchemy, to poetry and modern psychology.

In this important book, Patrick Harpur unpacks the myths that surround the soul. He explains that, once we have a clear understanding of this invisible yet vital part of ourselves, we will be well on our way towards answering many of our questions about existence, human nature and our place in the universe.

ISBN 9781846041860

Order this title direct from www.riderbooks.co.uk

The Boy Who Saw True

by Anon

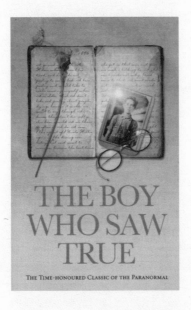

The Boy Who Saw True is based on the diary entries of a young Victorian boy whose extraordinary supernatural talent reveals itself within these pages. By turns naïve, insightful, funny and moving, it is an extremely convincing account of a precocious paranormal talent, and all the more persuasive because the young diarist never sets out to win over his readers. Born with incredible clairvoyant powers, the anonymous author could see auras and spirits, yet failed to realise that other people were not similarly gifted. This remarkable book has become a paranormal classic.

ISBN: 9781844131501

Order this title direct from www.riderbooks.co.uk

Testimony of Light

An extraordinary message of life after death

by Helen Greaves

When Frances Banks died her friend Helen Greaves was by her side. Then, one evening, some three weeks after Frances's death, Helen sensed her presence. This extraordinary encounter marked the beginning of contact between them from either side of the veil.

Testimony of Light is based on the communications that Helen received telepathically from Frances. The scripts have been authenticated by those who knew them both. Moving and inspiring, this book is a testament to the enduring power of their friendship and offers an important message to us all – that the death of the body is but a gentle passing to a much freer and fuller life.

ISBN: 9781844131358

Order this title direct from www.riderbooks.co.uk

Watching Over Us

What the Spirits Can Teach Us About Life

James Van Praagh

Bestselling author James Van Praagh is the celebrity medium whose work is a major inspiration behind the hit TV show *Ghost Whisperer*. During his international career as a messenger of the spirit world, he has been amazed by how involved the spirits are in our daily lives. Our loved ones may have passed over, yet they still care.

In *Watching Over Us*, Van Praagh shares shocking and emotional stories which show how keen the spirits are to help us learn from their mistakes, and to send messages to those left behind. This is a life manual with a difference, full of wisdom from the Other Side …

ISBN: 9781846042164

Order this title direct from www.riderbooks.co.uk

An Angel to Guide Me

How Angels Speak to Us from the Beyond

Glennyce Eckersley

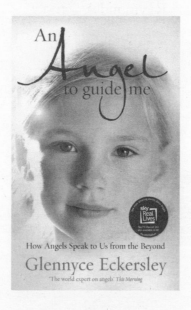

Glennyce Eckersley is one of our most loved angel experts. In *An Angel to Guide Me*, she explains how angels communicate with us through the five senses of sight, hearing, smell, taste and touch, as well as the mysterious sixth sense of intuition.

Amazing true stories collected from around the world show how many of us have had incredible angelic experiences that appear to have been tailor-made for us, speaking to us through the senses in the ways we understand the best. These stories are illustrated by exercises, affirmations and quotations, which will help you too to connect with the angels who care for you.

ISBN 9781846041600

Order this title direct from www.riderbooks.co.uk

The Light Beyond

The Extraordinary Sequel to the
Classic Bestseller Life After Life

Raymond A. Moody

What happens when we die? In his groundbreaking work *Life After Life*, Dr Raymond Moody pioneered research into the 'near-death experience' or NDE. In this, his stunning sequel, he explores how many NDE survivors have uncannily similar stories to tell, and considers what their extraordinary stories can teach us.

Engaging with witnesses from medicine, psychiatry and sociology, Dr Moody asks challenging questions about provides intriguing answers to those who wonder about dying. His message is provocative yet offers a reassuring glimpse of hope from the frontier between life and death.

ISBN: 9781844135806

Order this title direct from www.riderbooks.co.uk

JOIN THE RIDER COMMUNITY

Visit us online for competitions, free books, special offers, film clips and interviews, author events and the latest news about our books and authors:

R www.riderbooks.co.uk

 Rider Books on Facebook

 @Rider_Books

blog riderbooks.tumblr.com

RIDER BOOKS, 20 VAUXHALL BRIDGE ROAD, LONDON SW1V 2SA
E: INFO@RIDERBOOKS.CO.UK